CONTENT

Introduction xv

My Birth Forecast 1
People Got Scared 2
Miracle Child 3
After Birth.. 4
Guru Nanak.. 5
Being Invisible 7
Telepathy 8
Nanak Sar 9
Baba Isher Singh.. 10
Baba Sadhu Singh.. 12
Future Forecast 13
Joining 'The Way to God'.. 14
Fubi Kants.. 16
Healing by the Master 'Live' 18
Nectar 18
Moment to Moment 'Live' 19
European Seminar 'Live' 20
Elvis Presley 20
Spine 21
Pearl is Out 'Soul' 22
Deep Samadhi 'Live'...23

PinPoint Attention 'Live' 24

Attention 3rd Eye 25

Being at Two Places 'Live' 26

Paul Ji of East 27

Feelings 'Live' 27

Chosen for Master-ship 29

God Send You Back to Me 'Live' 29

Yabal Sakabi Ji 30

European Seminar 31

Future 32

Master-ship 33

Banjani Ji 33

Healings 34

Balance 'Live' 36

Inner 37

Nanak Sar Temple 37

Borrowed Vision 'Live' 38

Spiritual Master Agreed 39

European Seminar-Norway 41

Decision 42

Buzzing Bees 'Live' 43

Work Hard 43

I Am Shy 43

Moon Flight 'Live' 44

My Self 45

Spiritual Eye 45

The Way to God 46

Eldest of All 47

Towart Monagi 48

The Will of God

My Golden journey

SHER GILL Galib

Grosvenor House
Publishing Limited

This book is published by
Grosvenor House Publishing Ltd
Link House
140 The Broadway, Tolworth, Surrey, KT6 7HT.
www.grosvenorhousepublishing.co.uk

A CIP record for this book
is available from the British Library

Paperback ISBN 978-1-80381-238-0
Hardback ISBN 978-1-80381-238-0
eBook ISBN 978-1-80381-240-3

First Published: 03-09-2014

Website: www.shergill.uk.com
Email: beingasaint@gmail.com

SHER GILL Galib

Representing Golden Book 48

Little Golden Deer 49

Telepathy 'Live' 49

Telepathy 'Live' 50

Sadhu 'Saint' 51

Lower Worlds 51

Future Spiritual Master 52

Cloak of God-Man 52

Baba Nand Singh 53

Heart Chakra 'Live' 53

Word of God 54

The Journey 55

Golden Hair 56

Healer 56

Father got Healings 56

Healing for a Friend 57

Kal's Trap 'Live' 58

Past Life 59

Past Life 60

Past Life 60

More Training 61

Paul & I are One 62

Hairbreadth of Difference 'Paul Ji' 63

Paul Ji's Book 64

God-Realisation 65

Politics 65

Guru Gobind Singh Ji 66

Body 66

To See God in 5 Seconds 'Live' 67

Sai Baba 67

Monthly Report 'Copy' 68

The Answer 69

The Light 70

Baba Balak Nath 'Live' 70

My Village 71

Direct Projection 72

Para-Vidya 73

Para-Vidya 'All night' 74

Spirit 75

Guardian Angel 76

Soul Plane 76

Coins of Gold 77

New Man 'Myself' 77

Mysterious 78

Higher Initiations 78

Satsang 79

Alakh Lok – 6th Plane 79

Alaya Lok – 7th Plane 80

Hakikat Lok – 8th Plane 81

Residence of Master 'Live' 81

European Seminar - 31-7-1980 82

Agam Lok – 9th Plane 83

God Realisation 83

Concert 84

Prior to Worldwide 85

Spiritual Name 86

Master-ship 86

IKK-SAR 86

My Talk 87

Haiome Chants 88

Baba Budah Ji 88

Anami Lok 89

New Master. Worldwide 1981 91

Man in Waiting 'India' 93

The Big Answer 94

God-Man 30-3-1982 95

Taking over 96

Visit of Paul and Dapren 96

Visit of Satnam Ji 97

Monthly Report 98

Sedona Arizona 99

Future 1986 100

Guidance from Paul Ji 100

God on line 101

A Jogy 'Sage' 101

God Promise 102

Super Souls 102

Next God-Man 103

God-Man 103

Dapren & Braham 104

Rebazar Tarz 105

Master-ship Changed 106

Paul Ji 106

Paul Ji 107

Neutral 'Nowadays' 107

The Fees 108

Two Robes 108

Wind of Change 109

Taking over again 110

Future Delayed 111

Decision 112

Togetherness 113

Invasion from another Planet 113

Triad 115

God's Consent 115

Prophet 116

Paul Ji Visits 'Live' 116

Fed up in this World 116

Difficulties of Master 117

New Living Master 118

Letter to Dapren 119

The Gurus & Granth 122

Para-Vidya 'Live' 123

Meditation & Satsang 123

Mission 124

Normal 125

Mission Continues 126

Mission or Submission 127

God, Myself & a Child 130

The Message of 3 Giants 131

Negative Spirit 131

Uncompleted Mission 132

Purity 133

New Corporation 134

By – Law 134

Seeker's experience 134

Dapren in London 135
Present Situation 136
Depression Time 136
God's Blessings 137
Grand Father 138
Two Chakras 138
British Passport 139
Three Reminders 139
All Saints 140
Baba Isher Singh 140
European Seminar 141
House in Heaven 141
The Time 142
Spirit 143
Future Destruction 144
Good Feeling 144
Goal 145
The Voice 145
Flying Poster 146
The walk 147
I am getting old 147
Sadness 148
Change of dates 148
Manifestation 149
Spirit at work 149
The book 150
Goodbye 151
You can't hide 151
Light 152

Light 153

Start working 153

Last two Initiations 154

Next Paul Ji 154

The Will of God 155

Upgrading 155

Mrs Satwant Kaur 156

Big house 156

Time is short 157

Time up 157

I Nodded Yes 158

Hovering Paul Ji 158

Paul Ji & Psychic 159

Experiences 159

Another experience 160

Rani came to our house 160

Morning 161

Spiritual Responsibility 161

Voice of God 162

Monthly Report 163

Spiritual Mantle Picture 164

Darshan Manic 165

Rude Awakening 165

Darwin Leaving Stage 166

Darwin & Three Masters 168

Sher Gill & Spiritual Mantle 169

October 2008 169

Thank You, Seekers 170

'God' 171

God's World 172

The Way to God 173

Spirit 175

State of Consciousness 175

I am always with you 176

You will never see God 181

Satnam Ji 'Live' 182

Satnam Ji.. 183

Enlightenment.. 184

Rude Awakening 2 188

Spiritual Terminology.. 191

INTRODUCTION

Since young, I have been writing my diary. That is to note any outstanding spiritual experiences as they occurred in my life. Although I have seen over a thousand experiences, I managed to write over two hundred in this diary. All experiences are unique, written with dates as they occurred; The title of each experience was chosen as I felt within. So please accept the writings as they are.

I am sure this book will encourage many spiritual Seekers. A few experiences are published in my first book, 'The Way to God' as they were part of my spiritual training. They will remain part of this book; as this is my original diary. Spirit was so live with me at times; I was not sure if I was operating Physically or Spiritually. My soul body was so awakened; Spirit did most of my physical tasks.

The physical body was just an excuse to touch something. My spiritual journey began at a very young age; Spirit gave the experience of my spiritual life to my family. I recommend reading this book to glimpse my spiritual journey. This journey leads me to dwell within the heart of God. This should be the ultimate goal of every spiritual Seeker.

Many Seekers of different faiths strive to have one glimpse of the spiritual world. My book will act as proof for them to know that it is possible; if one puts in enough effort and has a spiritual teacher to lead them. Many claim to show the way; you will find that they are all pseudo masters.

Nowadays, people are not as illiterate, so you cannot lead them with blind faith.

It is a scientific world; people demand proof of your travels and ask if you can show them how to achieve this spiritual experience. This is also the answer to those who say, 'God does not exist' I have proved this to myself, so can they. This journey is within; it can take place in the physical too. For this reason; At places, I have used the word **live** next to the title of the experience. The Spirit is beyond limits.

The crux of the matter is; 'Can you do it or not? 'Have you seen it or not? In many cases, non-believers become firm followers. You never know what could touch their hearts. My spiritual journey expresses what faith, patience, silence and all the virtues of God is. We must adopt several of God's qualities to become the assistants of God. This is my golden Journey in God's world; it could be yours. My best wishes to all who want to discover the ocean of love and mercy here and now.

SHER GILL Galib

MY BIRTH FORECAST
11-3-1953

My grandmother was a follower of saint Nand Singh of Nanak Sar. Two days before my birth, on 11 March 1953 at 4 am, he appeared alongside her bed. However, he had passed away from the physical on 29 August 1943. As she gathered to wake up, the saint said in Punjabi; **'Parso tuhade ghar boota lagana hai, us da khial rakhio. Us da muh kade ve nahi futkarna. Oh jo ve karega-theek karega. Janam toa baad sanu bhura bheta karna'.**

Translation; Someone special, a **Saint,** will be born in your house in two days-time. 'Never refuse what he says,' then he mentions my mission in life and his last words were; 'upon his birth, as a gift, provide us with a wool blanket.' A blanket is a symbol to honour someone. There was a deeper meaning behind it, which I may share in the future.

My grandmother was such that she could not wait for two days. As soon as this saint disappeared, she freshened herself by taking a bath and having a teacup. Luckily, she had a brand-new wool blanket in her possession. She walked to his temple, which is about 3 miles away, early in the morning. 'The rest of the family were wondering where she was? Around 8 am when she returned, the whole family asked this question, 'Where have you been?

She replied; Something good will happen; I will tell you when the right time comes. Anyone asked no further questions because she was the most trusted person in the family and the village. I was born on Friday at 4 am 13 March 1953, then she revealed her secret. As I grew up,

1

she also told most of the elder members of our family and me. Her experience was a great help to focus my thoughts on the spiritual side.

Thanks to my grandmother. I loved her dearly and she died in the mid-eighties. This experience will keep her alive as long as I live. Later: my father passed this information over to my eldest nephew in my presence before departing from this world.

PEOPLE GOT SCARED
13-3-1953

My grandmother must have thought of my name in advance or this saint told her. I am not sure, as she is not living to reveal this. At birth, she said, 'Sher has come' someone heard and got scared in the neighbourhood. The word passed in nearby houses; they looked for the 'Tiger' as my name means this in English. Someone asked, 'Where is the tiger? And finally, the word reached my grandmother's ear and she answered back to everyone.

'Sher dhur dargah toh aaya' Translation: Sher has come from heaven and everyone relaxed. After that, she revealed the secret as mentioned in the beginning. She told me this at a very early age and this gave me the spiritual direction to follow.

This is the house I was born in and spent my first fourteen golden years before coming to England. My great-grandfather built it in 1920. His name was Ranjit Singh Gill but people often called him 'Raja Ranjit Singh' Raja means king. This was the title given to him as he was wealthy and a generous man to the needy or poor. This house is in Village; Galib Kalan, District; Ludhiana, India.

MIRACLE CHILD
1958

I remember a super miracle when I was about five years of age. I was standing in the alleyway within our house. This alleyway is about 8 ft wide and a one-year-old child was lying almost naked, 'wearing a nappy' in the middle. I saw a bull running wild towards us, weighing about 900kg. I believe some men must have badly beaten this bull and due to that, he was trying to escape through our house. That is why he was running wildly.

Due to unknown reasons, I did not move an inch from my position; one hundred percent, I was not scared at all. This child was helpless to move anyway. The bull approached us at full speed and I could not help noticing the bull's front left foot stamp the middle of that child's stomach. 'Can you imagine the bull's weight in this wild situation?

To my surprise, as he passed us and went, there was not even a scratch on that child. There was something which I will never forget; during those few seconds of experience, all of the time, my visual focus, better known as the spiritual gaze, was on that child.

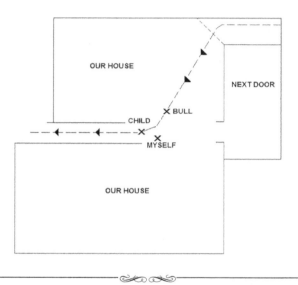

AFTER BIRTH
1958/9

My first six years of life were a strange experience. I did not speak for that time or period. I used only sign language to communicate. Some people thought I was born mute but everyone understood my signs. To be honest, I do not recall this memory. My mother has told me several times whenever a question comes up about someone's child who does not speak after one year. It seemed like maybe I did not want to speak with anyone. Many saints use sign language; I was good at that.

GURU NANAK
Year 1962

I had a beautiful experience with our first guru, 'Sri Guru Nanak.' Guru Nanak appeared and woke me up when I was sleeping in my bed. He led me to the place in our village as shown in the sketch. That must be about 600 yards away from my bed. There was a stage very similar to any theatre. Guru Nanak appeared on this stage and suddenly, he turned himself into a small child. I was looking at the stage as an audience, 'I was the only audience.'

Throughout this experience, the whole show was about the life of Guru Nanak. It was not anyone else performing but Guru Nanak himself. The entire experience was a night long. When the experience began, it was daytime and it was so colourful, totally out of this world. Guru Nanak appeared first; He was just born and then grew up into childhood. Then he appeared as a teenager and then his experience progressed to youth. Then middle age and eventually old age and finally his last few days.

This experience was similar to; he has shown me every day of his life until his last day in this world. On his last day, Guru Nanak vanished from the stage to heaven. I found myself lying in bed again but pondering upon what I had just seen or witnessed. Spirit is beyond limits, such as day or night and what it can create for any Seeker to experience. The experience was so live, as you go to any Theatre show during the day. I can still go over and over in my memory.

The Spirit very much blessed me and I am fortunate enough to experience the life of Guru Nanak. I am very thankful to Guru Nanak for appearing to me in this manner and at such a young age, approximately nine years. As you can see in the sketch, it was an empty plot of land at that time. At present, someone I know has built his house on that land. As in the photograph, I re-visited the place and stood on the spot where theatre stage was.

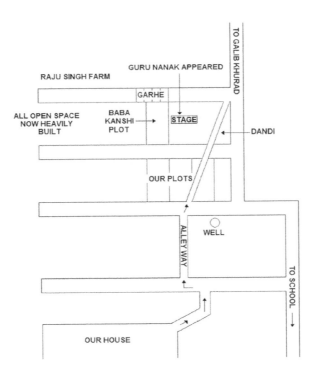

BEING INVISIBLE
age 12 years

I was playing catch-catch with my elder brother **Hardev** and cousin **Charan**. I was supposed to run in front so that they could catch me. There was an empty plot through which I made my plans to run away to escape but they had a better idea. They planned that one person would run behind me and the other would confront me from the opposite direction. In other words, they set up the trap and it worked.

I was caught in the middle of that empty plot of land, probably the size of 40 x 100 ft. I was standing in the middle and thinking I had been caught but they looked very disappointed and said to each other from opposite directions, 'Where has he gone? But I was standing right in the middle of that plot. One of them walked passed me, having given up. I could see them but they could not see me. To them, I was invisible at that moment.

'That instance I will never forget.'

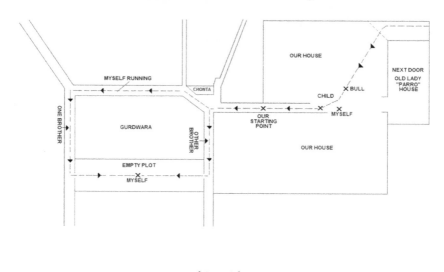

TELEPATHY
Ability at a young age

From a very young age in India, I had this telepathic ability. There was an old lady named **Parro;** she lived next door. Being my grandmother's best friend, she loved me a lot. She was the one who got scared at my birth and said, 'Where is the Tiger? She was also a devotee of Baba Nand Singh. People gave me the nickname' Fouzi' when I was young because of my looks and how I walked,' which means a soldier. She used to call me Fouzu.

Whenever she thought of me, I could hear physically she had called my name. I used to go and ask her if everything was okay. She always replied; Yes, I was thinking of you and I used to help her whenever she asked for it. After coming to England, I could hear her calling my name every 'Now and then.' She passed away around 1980; ever since I have never heard her. Thanks to her for having this pure love for me.

NANAK SAR
28-8-1963

Thanks to my grandmother's guidance, I knew my mission in this life from a very early age. I knew that my life would be lived on a spiritual basis. I was a regular visitor to this saint's temple, built-in 1950 onwards by his successor named saint Isher Singh. I had the privilege to be in his presence by standing next to him several times and listening to his spiritual discourses.

I will never forget the day; we were five or six boys standing in a particular corner (near Baran darri) when Isher Singh came near us, holding lots of sweet (yellow) rice in his possession. He began to give 'handfuls' to all the boys and I was standing right in front of him. He never gave me any rice because I was too busy looking at his face. 'That was the first time I came to know what is 'Noor? Noor means a spiritual countenance on someone's face.

So it was a treasure for me to hold on to.

BABA ISHER SINGH
6-10-1963

He passed away on 6 October 1963 at 7.30 pm, aged 46 years and I stood by his body, among other followers, for three days. On the third day, his body was taken to its final resting place at Hari Ke Pattan, Punjab. It was that time my grandmother gave me the mission to take food from our village to his temple every day in the evening time. She prepared the food 'Parshada' 'Chupatties and curry' and neatly placed it in the basket. It must be about 7/8 kg in weight.

I used to carry this over my head at the age of ten and then walked three miles every day in the evening and stayed there overnight. I listened to spiritual hymns and prayers at night-time and early in the morning and then walked home to attend school. I was given a (Kully) room of 5 x 6 feet to sleep in over winter and in summer, I used to sleep on paving bricks next to a water pool 'Sarowar.' A Saff was used to cover bricks. In English, Saff is made of 'Daabh' or known as Halfa grass or long-cordgrass.

My two cousins accompanied me now and then. This continued till 7 October 1967 and I came to England on 8 October 1967. Baba Nath was responsible for looking after me; he was an older man and a father figure to me. He accompanied Baba Isher Singh all his life as a right-hand man to play brass couplets 'Tallia.' He taught the art of Tallia to everyone interested in that temple. I attempted to learn as well.

In March 2014, **I re-visited** Nanak Sar temple to determine if my little room 'Kulli' still exists. Most of the old little rooms have been demolished and new buildings have been constructed. To my surprise, only two small rooms are kept by this temple on historical grounds. One of them is my old residence 5 x 6 feet Room. When I went there, it was locked and I inquired who would have the key.

I was told his name was Mr Mohinder Singh. I went to see him and explained that I used to occupy this little room one time. If he did not mind, I would like to go inside once more to refresh my old memories. He gave me the keys and I unlocked the door once more after 47 years and photos were taken with this gentleman. He told me that ever since I left this little room in 1967, he was given the key and authority to use it from 1968 up until today.

11

I had never met him before because he joined this temple in 1968. Originally this little room belonged to Baba Nath Ji mentioned in the above paragraph. He was given a new and much larger room as he grew old. I was given the key to staying to sleep or meditating during the night.

BABA SADHU SINGH

Every evening upon my arrival in that temple, Baba Sadhu Singh used to ask me if I was okay. I had heartfelt respect for this person. He was the main person standing next to Baba Isher Singh all the time as his assistant, better known as 'Hazooria' in Punjabi. He was the person to be in line for master-ship but it did not materialise for some reason.

12

The reasons were that Baba Isher Singh's physical journey was cut short, as he died at the age of only 46 years. Baba Sadhu Singh was not ready spiritually to take over when this unexpected situation occurred. After this, at least four people claimed the master-ship but none were eligible for this. This is a widespread practice in this world; the reasons are to gain power.

FUTURE FORECAST

One day I was standing at the x-spot indicated in the sketch and heard the voice. 'If you are looking for peace, there is plenty here but '**What**' you are looking for, you will not find here.' It was a clear indication for me to move on and seek somewhere else. This is not mentioned in my diary but now I will tell you what I was looking for. I wanted to have the same spiritual abilities as Baba Nand Singh and Isher Singh.

The forecast was correct because there was no one else to train me or reveal the secrets to materialise my goal. I was willing to go to any lengths or religion to achieve my goal. Spirit intervened and led me to the new path and my journey began in the spiritual worlds. I was shown a lot more than I expected. Also, it was revealed within a short period that I was in line for the master-ship on this path.

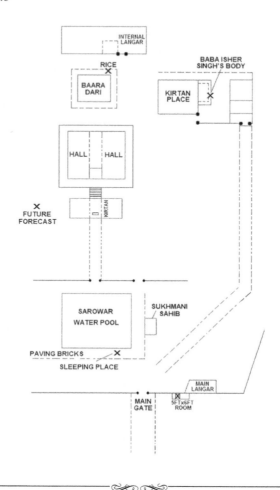

―――――――――――――― ✺❧ ――――――――――――――

JOINING 'THE WAY TO GOD'
26-9-1976

I used to work at the building site, 'John Mowlem' and met a lovely man Mr Manic one day. He was talking to someone about this path; who was not interested. I was standing a few feet away. 'Not interfering,' I could not help listening to what he said. Later I approached Mr Manic, if he could tell me what he was saying earlier. He was a new member on this path and upon request, he gave me a book written by Sri Paul Ji to read.

Most of the higher planes' explanation was very familiar as I read through them. I knew this is what I had been searching for. I said to Mr Manic, 'I want to join' following this, we met Mr P. Singh, who explained the teachings to me thoroughly and asked if I had any questions. He was a sincere and spiritually awakened person in the teachings. I said, 'I do not have questions' I filled in the joining form and enclosed a fee of $65- and bought the complete set of books written by Paul Ji.

Although physically, I joined on 26 September 1976, I have followed the same teachings since I was born. As I posted the joining letter in the mailbox at 96 South Road, Southall a strange experience began. Wherever I went, somebody invisible 'Spiritual Master' was with me. When I went to work, somebody went to work with me. When I worked, it worked with me; when I sat down, it sat down with me too. I could feel but I could not see.

Every time I looked around to catch it, I could not see anything. I often swung my arms in the air to catch but I could not but the spiritual Master was so close. He was nearer than my heartbeat. I was amazed by this experience. It was a wonderful experience to have someone with you in this manner. He is the best companion you can have in the whole world. Since then, the spiritual Master and I have never parted. It is the live experience from the Master when he said, I am always with you.

15

He means: What he says. 'You can prove this to yourself.'

Fubi Kants
10-11-1976

I remember my first **Initiation** given by Sri Fubi Kants, which took place at the Katsu-pari Monastery. My soul body woke up and I found myself in front of a big temple. I met somebody there and we shook hands. He led me into the temple, passing by the water pool, 'Sarowar' there was Fubi Kants. He showed me around the temple and asked me to watch a rather long film on the projector and screen.

It was about the spiritual history since Satya-Yuga. Sometimes I was in the film 'Where I was part of the history' sometimes I watched the movie. It was a very long story on a big screen in the hall. There were lots of other people or spiritual visitors in the hall.

I noticed somebody on the other side of the hall, lying on the floor. His body became radiant like snow-white 'sparkling stars' lighting in all directions. After a while, his body rose above the floor, up to the ceiling level and then down. Someone told me that he is practicing soul travel; I told him I would try as well.

Fubi Kants was watching. I lay on the floor but I could not do it. Then Fubi Kants gave me some instructions on doing soul travel and the big film carried on. It was a very action-packed film and the fastest film I have ever seen. After some trials, I managed to lift my soul body off the floor and it also turned into bright, brilliant stars, as mentioned earlier.

After my success, Fubi Kants said in Punjabi; 'Dekh meri darhi hunn kitanni chitti hai.' Translation; 'look how bright white is my beard' I felt he was proud of me. He was feeling the beard with his hands while talking to me. He looks very similar to the sketches done by someone. He is about my height, 5 ft 9 in. with a long beard and he was wearing white clothes and a turban at that time.

HEALING BY THE MASTER 'LIVE'
9-10-1976

I damaged my shoulder at work. It was slightly painful. Later that night, while I was sleeping, somebody woke me up without touching me. I looked at the ceiling and then sideways. I knew that someone was there but I could not see. Again, I looked properly at the ceiling and sideways. My inner was telling me that someone was there. When I turned around to the spot where my feelings were strong, I spotted someone.

Instantly that force made me unconscious and turned my body sideways, the affected shoulder in the upper position. After a while, that force brought me back into a semi-conscious state. Master was releasing the spiritual vibrations to the affected part. I could feel the warm and sensational vibrations given to the shoulder as a massage, during which I fell to sleep. When I woke up in the morning, the pain was gone and my shoulder was perfect.

NECTAR
22-10-1976

I was sleeping in my little room, 'Box room' at 43 Leamington Road, Southall, during the night, I woke up. I saw the drops of nectar 'Amrit' dripping from the right-hand side of the ceiling near my right-hand shoulder. Nectar looked so bright, it was inexplicable. Later I wished that I should have licked it. Spirit had blessed my little room.

I had spent at least 25 years in this little room. This is where I did my meditation and wonderful experiences took place. Although its volume was only 7ft x 9ft, being so small; 'Can you believe it used to open up according to our requirements? There are no limits in the dictionary of Spirit.

MOMENT TO MOMENT 'LIVE'
6-6-1977

Darwin is the present living Master and his spiritual name is Dapren, therefore we will use his spiritual name in this book.

A strange experience began in my life daily, moment to moment. I always felt, 'That I am Dapren,' while I was looking at something or in any direction or talking to someone. I lost my own physical identity. I was not trying to copy Dapren in any manner. But all the actions were coming automatically in a very natural way like we were breathing together. I was enjoying myself throughout the whole experience.

Now I have learned what it means when the Master says; As spiritual Master, I am close to your breath or heartbeat. That was the living proof of Masters' statement.

This is how close I am to Dapren.

In a sense, you become one; there is no difference between yourself and the Master. If you are so close to the Master, then there is no such miracle you cannot create.

❧❧

European Seminar 'Live'
15/17-7-1977

This year's European Seminar took place on 15/17 July 1977 in Brighton, England. This was the first time I met Master physically. It was a pleasure meeting him and I had some wonderful experiences at the seminar. I had about three live experiences. First experience; As I met him, we shook hands near the stage area of the hall. He looked into my eyes and I could see special rays of light coming from his eyes and penetrating my eyes. It is known as 'The Master's gaze' as soon as he let go of my hand, I found myself at the exit door of the hall; it must be about 80ft away.

❧❧

Elvis Presley
Morning papers on Wednesday 17-8-1977

I was a fan of Elvis Presley and at night, I had a dream. Elvis was singing on the stage and I watched him from the audience. The strange thing was that he was singing and doing all kinds of dancing moves as he used to do but no sound or voice was coming out of his mouth. When I woke up, I wondered why I had such a dream. Later in the morning, when I went to work, looking at the newspapers; It was the head news of the day on the front page of every paper. Elvis, king of 'Rock n Roll,' died at 42 on 16 August 1977.

King Elvis is dead or Elvis is no more.

SPINE
20-8-1977

This experience is for the people who are meditating while lying in bed. So this may be a way out. Paul Ji and I had some conversation on this subject then he showed me a special sofa bed. He asked me to bring it near to him so that he could teach me how to lay down for meditation.

It was specially made for this purpose. In this position, you are neither lying down nor sitting right up. The main objective is to keep the spine straight as much as possible.

PEARL IS OUT 'SOUL'
27-8-1977

Master said; This is an example of how to practice soul travel. How gently you should move out of your physical body. There was a plastic box. Inside the box, there was a pearl. He guided me to get this pearl out of the box with my imagination or willpower. After some practice, it popped out into my hand. I was thrilled.

It is a technique of doing soul travel, gentle, subtle and effortless as much as possible at the same time doing it.

DEEP SAMADHI 'LIVE'
5-9-1977

This question arises in the mind of new or old Seekers who have not been through this experience yet. This is a unique experience and will clear many doubts from those who believe that they fall asleep during their meditation. In the early days, I had my doubts and thought that I was wasting my time during meditation.

During meditation, I used to fall asleep the same as everyone else. I went to see someone who was more senior than I am in our spiritual teachings. The answers I received from this person were not very satisfactory. I came home a little disappointed. Somehow, I knew that there was more to it than sleep. My evening meditation time was approaching; I thought, why not ask the spiritual Master. At the beginning of meditation, I requested to clear up this point.

I began meditation, as usual and after a while, I fell asleep again. This time spiritual Master woke me up and made me conscious enough physically to know what was happening within. While I was still in the middle of the experience, What I witnessed was totally 'Amazing'. My mouth was shut entirely but the word I was chanting at the beginning of meditation was rolling within.

It was on a continuous roll with such a rhythm without fail. I wished to keep on listening but he retook me into meditation when the Master knew I was satisfied. Your word begins to chant itself without making any physical or mental effort. This is called true meditation or better known as **Deep Samadhi** in India.

This happens when you are doing spiritual exercise with complete sincerity. It is an effortless effort and all your mental activities vanish. With the blessings of your Master, everything is possible. 'Without the Master, who would you request to? or 'Who will wake you up during the middle of meditation to show what is taking place?

These are three stages of meditation.

1. In the beginning, you are trying to chant spiritual word. You are conscious of this repetition and also the surrounding noises. A few thoughts are still wandering around.

2. You go into a rhythm and your thoughts and surrounding noises vanish.

3. You become unaware of yourself physically. This rhythm stops vocally and the word repeats itself within on a continuous roll until you become conscious of yourself again. Or the Master gives you the nudge meaning the time is up.

This Is Deep Samadhi

PINPOINT ATTENTION 'LIVE'
10-10-1977

I am always trying to find new or easy ways of doing soul travel and Master is always here to help. Today I was doing my meditation and the Master came and pointed at my spiritual eye. He touched my forehead with his thumb and said; It is no use in fixing a drawing pin here. He said to move around in your imagination. When Master knows that you are trying, he is always here to guide you.

ATTENTION 3ᴿᴰ EYE
12-11-1977

Spiritually I am excellent but not as good as I wanted to be; no matter how much you know, there is always a plus point to achieve. I have always tried to polish up my abilities further. I requested the Master to show me properly how to put my attention during the spiritual exercise. He appeared during the meditation and showed me how to pay attention to the third eye. He said; Put all your mental faculties or total 'Awareness' on the spiritual eye in an oblique manner while slightly pulling your attention in reverse order.

'Known as Effortless Effort'

This is where most of the Seekers are failing. First, they do not bother to put enough effort; secondly, they put too much strain on the 'Third-Eye' and try to penetrate through the forehead screen.

BEING AT TWO PLACES 'LIVE'
3-4-1978

During the birth of my elder son, I went to Hillingdon Hospital to be with my wife. The visiting hours were from 4.30 to 5 pm and 6.30 to 8 pm. I did not have my car, so I decided to go early to have two visits. I went to the bus stop; the bus did not come for a long time. When I reached the hospital, the nurse told me, 'You are too late for the first visit; you have to wait now.' I said to myself; Tough luck. I sat on the chair in the waiting room.

I chanted my spiritual word 'Silently' to pass the time. I was chanting for a little while; then, I opened my eyes. There were other four people and some children making a fair amount of noise. I got up from that chair to another one in the corner. I looked through the big glass window and watched the clouds in the sky and some higher Hospital buildings.

I closed my eyes again for a short time, 'I was fully conscious,' then suddenly I woke up in my soul body. I travelled beyond the buildings and roamed near the clouds with my eyes fully open. But at the same time, I was fully conscious of the noise made by children in the waiting room. This noise was not interfering with my experience. This is what it means when the Master says;

'You can be in two places at the same time.'

PAUL JI OF EAST
21-5-1978

In this experience, I was shown the past lives of Paul Ji. I am thankful to the Spirit and feel blessed to have this knowledge. I noticed that he worked in the east for most of his past life. You can feel this within his writings too. Since he had been serving God's cause in the past, he is the spiritual mantle holder today.

FEELINGS 'LIVE'
4-6-1978

I used to assist Mr Manic with his meeting and we used to display posters in the shops to advertise the public meetings. One day we were in the High street, Southall and I began to feel something within myself. Every time we approached any shop, this feeling was telling me whether to display the poster in this shop or not.

We approached the chosen shop to display the poster. If Spirit said to me go in, we went in and the shopkeeper accepted the poster. Sometimes we wanted to display the poster at some shop but my Inner 'Message' told me, don't go in. I listened and told Mr Manic not to bother. He was such a character, if he wanted to do something, he would not listen and we were refused.

We went from shop to shop and every time I told him in advance, either this shop would accept or reject our poster. After a while, he realised that whatever I was telling him came hundred percent true. After this realisation he gave me lots of respect and said many times, I know, you have something spiritually which I don't. But I could not tell him that I am an open channel for Spirit. Since that day, this spiritual knowingness has stayed with me forever.

CHOSEN FOR MASTER-SHIP
7-6-1978

This was the first experience that indicated that I am in line for the master-ship after Dapren. We were in a village and somebody invited us for a drink. Master and I were walking together and other people were following us. I introduced other people to Master as I was the well-known person in the village. Mr P. Singh never turned up but all these people were also saints.

Master recommended that we all race to find out who is the best. Race is a symbol to differentiate the best in a state of consciousness. We all ran together. Master was the first one to complete the race and I came second. I was told what it means, that I am next in line for master-ship after Dapren. It was a long and wonderful experience.

GOD SEND YOU BACK TO ME 'LIVE'
9-6-1978

I was working at Crown Cork factory, Southall. I received my pay packet on Friday. According to my work, my habit was to look at the payslip to check if the amount 'Pounds sterling' was correct. I always counted the money without opening the pay packet because it is stapled. This week, my Inner told me to open the pay packet properly and check.

I said to myself, 'Why not? I checked all of the five-pound notes 'as they were all five pounds notes anyway' on one of them; something was written. That was the message from the Master.

'God Send You Back to Me; Darwin'

This was the second spiritual nudge for me to prepare myself to be the next in line for master-ship. I still have this old £5-note with me as a souvenir.

YABAL SAKABI JI
27-6-1978

This was a very long experience. I was taken there by the Master during my second Initiation to a spiritual city known as **Agam-Desh**. We met Sri Yabal Sakabi and he showed me all around the Temple. He was leading the way all the time, being In-charge and I was following him with Master.

Yabal Sakabi told us so many things for information. This Temple is almost underground. Then at the end of his spiritual discourse, he led the way for us; it was a long staircase leading to the ground level. We came out and I noticed the colour of the ground was maroon or very similar to gravel brick colour.

We were standing outside and Yabal Ji was still providing lots of spiritual knowledge and most of the time, I was on the listening end. It was a very pleasant experience, full of beyond knowledge.

He is slim built about 5 ft 8 inches tall to describe him. He was wearing a maroon colour robe. I was following him along all day and watched him quite closely. I noticed he hardly had any hair on his head, which may be about ten hairs.

His face is very similar to a friend of mine living in slough. I have seen some sketches made by someone but they are not as close as he looks but some reflection is there.

EUROPEAN SEMINAR
Germany 7/9-7-1978

During the seminar at Aachen, I desired to meet the Master somewhere while walking around the seminar hall. It did not happen physically but the spiritual Master appeared in the same hall on the Inner. We had a chat for a long time and I felt joy.

'My desire was fulfilled, thank you, Master'

FUTURE
1978

Experience; I was revealed the future of my uncle Mr K. S. During this experience, a known friend Mr M. S. was saying to me that his father had died. I kept silent but his father was admitted to the hospital; I felt he was not coming home anymore. I felt very concerned. Later, the Spirit told me that he would not die until I visited him. So I kept delaying my visit purposely. The family relationship was such that I should have gone much earlier.

I had to go and see him, so I decided to visit him with another person known as Bhag Singh one day. We went to see him in Hammersmith Hospital; the man appeared fine on our visit. I thought he didn't look like someone who was going to die. He was a fascinating person, quite jolly and looking forward to life. During our chat which lasted an hour, the man talked about his future of settling in India. He would buy one rifle and a pistol and he had saved enough money to see him through.

On the other hand, I knew that he had only a few more days left of his present life. He looked very healthy and full of life and a future to live for on that particular day. I felt his attachment to the physical and learned a few things for myself. The things that we aim for in life don't materialise. 'Two weeks later, he died.'

MASTER-SHIP
2-11-1978

Ever since I have known myself, I have wanted to be a holy man. Later I was sure that I was going to be a saint. When I first joined 'The Way to God,' I knew that I was in some kind of training and would be a saint. I thought that Master would train me, then probably send me on a mission to lead one of the popular religions in India. This year, I learned that I had been chosen to become the spiritual Master of this path.

Ever since I have been getting extraordinary experiences unavailable to other Seekers. Now I know why I have been different from everybody else. Since young, even now, I have been different. I do not think and act like others even today; I feel and think differently from the masses.

'I have been lonely but never alone.'

BANJANI JI
11-11-1978

In this experience, Master and I meet with **Banjani Ji** in the Gobi Desert at the border of Mongolia and China. It was a special Satsang we attended with Banjani Ji. He was expressing a spiritual message through his eyes '**Gaze.**'

At that time, he had a black/grey beard and slightly longer hair combed back. He was wearing a very simple but very neat robe of white or touch grey colour.

In the Satsang we were only five members. Banjani Ji told me that this is a very special Satsang and that only five people are allowed to attend at a time, only the privileged ones. I was pleased to be in that Satsang. Whenever I remember that experience, I always feel blessed. Banjani Ji has a charming smile. I have a picture of him made by someone and it is 90 percent accurate and matches the description. Again he is about 5 ft 7 in, tall with Indian looks.

HEALINGS
19-12-1978

My friend did not turn up to pick me up while going to work in 1975. He was my best friend and beyond trust. I waited at the **spot** where he used to pick me up every day in his car, so I waited and waited for one and half hours. Finally, I decided to catch a bus and go to work. But during that waiting period, I thought and thought. I was shocked; after a while, the pain started in the back of my head, just above the neck area. It increased every day. I tried all types of painkillers given by my Doctor but the pain increased even more.

Since that day, I stopped talking to my friend. We parted without a single word from each other. I suffered that pain for over three years. In the winter of 1978, another friend went to India for his holidays. He gave me the keys to his flat Ref; 00 Hortus road, Southall, so I could look after it for him. I used to go there every evening for a routine security check. There was a Christian Church almost next to the flat. That church had a signboard in the front yard it reads;

Clairvoyance on: Thursday
Healings on: Friday

Luckily: It was Friday, so it was Healing day. At that time, I was not aware of any pain. I just wanted to go inside to have a look around. As you noticed, anything to do with spiritualism has been my interest in life. I went inside and they were giving healing to two ladies by rubbing their particular painful areas and talking to them simultaneously. I could not hear a word. There were not many people inside. I kept watching and thinking about if they asked me what I wanted, then what would I say to them; just before my turn, I slipped outside.

When I came out, I suddenly realised my pain and said to myself; you need healings to your neck. I stood outside the church to decide; 'Should I go back inside or not? Then realisation came from within. I said to myself, 'You have a great Master; why not write a letter to him? While I was walking home, I made up my mind to write a letter before sleeping. At night time I forgot about the letter and went to sleep.

When I woke up in the morning, the pain was gone completely; I knew that Master had healed me. The pain never returned since.

Moral: You don't have to write to the Master; he knows.

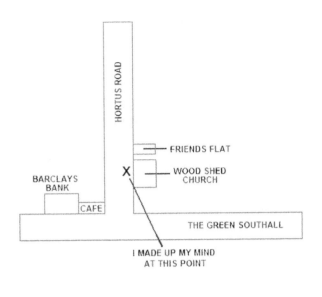

BALANCE 'LIVE'
1-2-1979

I used to stay out of balance most of the time as I had been busy spiritually and there was so much to take and digest. At the same time, I could not relate to any friends or people because I lived in my private world. After over two years following 'The Way to God' One day, I discovered that I am in balance. Since that day, I have been in balance most of the time.

INNER
17-3-1979

I had an experience with my foreman and two fellow workers while working on the machine. I told my foreman that I would like to shake hands with the spiritual Master.

The foreman replied; Your record shows you already have had a handshake with him. I replied; Yes but I would like to do it again.

Moral: It shows that we travel with the Master in the Inner but may not be aware as much on the outer.

NANAK SAR TEMPLE
5-4-1979

I requested Spirit to let me know who will be the next Master at Nanak Sar, as there were 4 / 5 people claiming to be the Masters. I met Baba Isher Singh Ji, the previous Master, during the night time he said to me in Punjabi.

'Agar Ihnaa Which Kush Hove, Ta Hun Nu Koi Gaddi Utte Baitth Na Janda'

'Exact words'

Translation: If any one of them had any spiritual power, they would have become the Master by now. He showed me the true spiritual status of these people claiming to be the Masters.

Later comment: This claiming of master-ship is not only in this path; it is everywhere.

BORROWED VISION 'LIVE'
March onwards 1979

My friend, Mr G. Singh had a car accident on the M1 motorway. Both of his eyes were severely damaged, especially the left eye. The windscreen smashed into small pieces and glass went inside his both eyes. The left eye was ultimately damaged. I went to see him at Watford Hospital because we were very close friends and had close family relations. He knew that I was following a spiritual Master, so he asked me if I could request him to get help.

I requested the Master for help during my evening meditation. I also used to take small naps (learned earlier) to get instant guidance from the Master. I received the consent and I promised that my Master would help him. The senior surgeon operated on both of his eyes. The doctor called me and his younger brother Mr M. Singh to his flat offered us tea and told us the total damage. He said that he had removed everything from his left eye. The doctors' flat was within the Hospital compound.

Mr Singhs' right eye is also severely damaged but later on, he would not have a hundred percent vision but he would have seventy percent vision, which is now confirmed. So, Mr Singh could not see anything from his left eye when the bandages were removed. But he could see a shadow vision through his right eye. But the doctor had told us that he would soon develop a cataract in his right eye.

The doctor said; that it would take at least three months to develop a cataract before he could remove it entirely. He did not want to discuss the left eye because he had already told us the condition. After a few days, the vision from his right eye began to disappear as the cataract began to develop. Mr Singh got scared as his world was turned into darkness. He was disappointed and depressed and began to cry over my shoulder.

He asked; if my Master could help him see through his left eye while the cataract was developing in the right eye. Mr Singh was not aware of his left eye condition because we never told him or the doctor. We did not want to break his heart. But anyway, I got a bit emotional and said I would ask him if he could give him the 'sight' for that period until his right eye begin to see again.

SPIRITUAL MASTER AGREED

So, as the shadowed vision disappeared from the right eye, the vision began to appear in his left eye. Later the vision from his right eye disappeared entirely but there was enough vision in the left eye. After discharge, we had a follow-up appointment with the leading surgeon who initially operated. I went with Mr G. Singh as an interpreter as usual. When our turn came, the doctor called us in. He checked his right eye and remarked; Blah-Blah, that his cataract was developing okay.

Then I broke the news to the doctor and said, doctor, 'Do you know, this man can see through his left eye? 'Can you imagine the doctor's face? It got red and he said to me, showing both of his hands, palms up, I have removed everything from his left eye with these two hands. 'How can he 'Possibly' see from his left eye? I said; okay, okay. But I put the challenge on the doctor to test his left eye. He agreed and tested his vision and Mr G. Singh read the big letters in no time. 'The doctor was shocked but never raised the question to know how?

The doctor was pleased; he gave him the thickest glasses so that he could see and Mr G. Singh began to see even better. He walked the streets of Southall, Middx, without any assistance or stick for a good three months. His cataract developed fully and the same surgeon removed the cataract and after a few days, his vision began to re-appear in his right eye properly and began to disappear from his left eye. He never saw again from his left eye.

That was a gift from the Master. During that period, I received spiritual guidance daily and moment to moment. The guidance was shared with Mr Singh and his family regarding when, date, time and what would happen. Every day's guidance came true a hundred percent and even more. Now you can count the number of days and the number of experiences I or we had.

'Can you imagine what we learned during that period? 'Can you imagine what Spirit is all about and what it can do?

Everything was done with a hundred percent faith in the Spirit. We can move the mountains with faith. It was total reliance upon Spirit. It Just Is.

Thank You

This experience was published in E. M. Journal 1979 – Volume 4 under; 'A call for help' on page 35. I have this copy in my file. During 1979 I was so busy with this person, so hundreds of experiences went unrecorded in this diary. Sometimes Seekers complain that their requests are not materialising when they request for someone. They want to see miracles but do not want to contribute to materialise these miracles.

During this miracle, I offered the Spirit that I would take any pain of this gentleman but we would help him. 'Which I did' Everyone is fascinated by these miracles but no one is willing to take any pain. If you are prepared, Spirit is Here. Jesus Christ or other saints, how much pain they used to take on behalf of their followers, you cannot even imagine. All you see is that miracle has taken place but you will only know the true value when you experience this pain in your body.

EUROPEAN SEMINAR-NORWAY
17/19-8-1979

This was another excellent seminar. I and Mr M. Singh, related to the above experience 'Borrowed Vision' especially went to this seminar to thank Dapren. But due to some circumstances, he did not come. So we said thank you to one of his team members. He sent Mr Harold Klemp as a guest speaker in his place. He was a fascinating man and made us laugh by telling us the story of a man who had a dream to build a church.

Story as told: He wondered if I build a church who will buy but good luck to him, somebody bought the church and he made some money. Then Spirit gave him another dream to build a bigger church and so he did; he made more money. The conclusion was; Listen to the Spirit and it works wonders. Everyone was happy to hear this exciting story. Later I managed to talk with this gentleman in the same seminar hall. He is the present leader of E......... organisation.

DECISION
9-9-1979

Due to lack of work, there was redundancy, where I was working at Crown Cork, Southall. I just could not make up my mind. I requested the Spirit for guidance.

Spirit said; 'Pick up your money' So I did.

Spirit knows best because the future of that factory was dull. This experience may not be that important to some in a mutual sense but it shows that the Spirit is always here to help. You only have to ask. Later that factory closed down.

BUZZING BEES 'LIVE'
11-9-1979

I was lying in bed but awake, near to the sleep state. Then I heard the sound of buzzing bees near my ears. When I heard it, instantly, my vibrations were raised very high. I closed my eyes to keep listening. I was nearly out of my body and concentrated on my spiritual eye. I could see the Master but the vision was not very clear, it was similar to someone standing in the fog. 'But I knew it was him'

WORK HARD
17-9-1979

This was guidance from the Master, we were working together and he was my supervisor. As a worker, I tried to be friendly with him, knowing that he was my spiritual Master. But instead, he stared at me and wanted me to carry on with my work. It shows that I should work hard spiritually and not take it lightly.

I AM SHY
19-9-1979

During my training, I was doubtful if I would be able to talk in front of an audience. Then Master appeared in a dream state. We were sitting in the cafe and chatting about this particular subject.

Master said; I used to think in the same manner.

A few days later, continuing from the above thought and experience. I was sitting on the stage with my mouth open and Spirit was doing the talking.

Conclusion: I will be the channel; Spirit will take over.

MOON FLIGHT 'LIVE'
27-9-1979

This is an extraordinary experience created during meditation. Master took me on a journey as accurate as it can be physically. We had a rocket and Master chose me as one of the crew. He asked me to take a position on the steering wheel.

Master was guiding and showing me some of the stars. He said, 'Keep your steering straight,' as there was a line of stars. We made a big circle going from one planet to another, all the Solar system and the Galaxy of stars and finally we landed on the Moon. He gave all the details as we went from one planet to another.

MY SELF

This is my personal view. As you have read about my childhood, I wanted to lead a saintly life. So to get married was totally out of the question. There was lots of family pressure over the last few years and I gave up. My daughter taught me what love force is all about. In other words, she helped me to come down to this earth planet. Otherwise, I was not interested in this world or its relations, titles or materialism.

Later, I learned that I had been grounded in this life with material shackles by saying, 'Yes' once to married life. The outcome is unwanted pain and obstructions in my spiritual endeavours. The Spirit and Kal force had used these tools known as a family to chain me down to this earth. Otherwise, these two forces knew that I would be uncontrollable spiritually or by anyone. Later, I discovered many more secrets used by Spirit to keep me under control.

SPIRITUAL EYE
5-10-1979

I used to take a public meeting in Maidenhead central library and a young man used to come there. His name was Mr Alan; after attending a few sessions with me, he joined 'The Way to God.' One day he came to the meeting as usual.

No one else came on that day, so he told me about an incredible experience he had with me.

He said he was doing his meditation, then suddenly I 'Sher Gill' appeared in his spiritual eye and began to give him rather a long talk in some other language. Alan said; he understood every word that I said to him during that time but after the experience, he forgot what I said when he became conscious.

Spirit's grace gave me the privilege to appear in someone's spiritual eye. Thank You.

THE WAY TO GOD
7-10-1979

Experience; I was looking for a job and went into one big hall for an interview. There were many other people and one lady was interviewing everyone. She wanted people to do so many jobs. Everyone had their interview and they all accepted one or two subjects on which they could teach or lecture.

At last, my turn came when I was asked, 'What subject will I choose? I said 'The Way to God' and that one subject will be enough for me to lecture on. Then I was told that, If I am going to lecture on God, we will pay you to double the money you are getting now. I said, 'Thank you.'

ELDEST OF ALL
21-10-1979

Experience; The Spiritual Master took me back into the past to show my previous lives, as he had done on many occasions. He said this might interest you more than any other re-incarnation you had on this earth. He said this was the beginning of the human race on earth. Then he let me slip into the experience to see what it was and how it all began.

Five of us 'Men' came down from heaven or God. As we approached the earth, we were in a standing position. It was no different than how we stand today. Coming down from heaven to earth was very similar to as we jump with a parachute to the ground but landing very gently. The greenery of this earth was awesome, breathtaking or very similar to heaven. So, we landed 'feet' first and made our mark. God thoroughly prepared the earth for human inhabitants. So I was one of the first five people to reach here.

We five must have been very close to God, so it decided to send us first. That was the beginning of Satya-Yuga or the Golden-Age. It clearly shows that I have been here, on this earth planet, longer than anybody else. This is why; I never agreed with the scientific theory that we progressed from monkey species. We are one 'Human' creation among 84 hundred thousand. I'm afraid I have to disagree with make-believe theories. Nor do I agree with mythological stories. I believe in something, whether it **Is** or **Not**.

TOWART MONAGI
22-10-1979

He is one of our spiritual Master from this unbroken line of Masters since Satya-Yuga; his background is from Africa. He served his time as living Master of this path long ago. One day Master took me into the past to meet him so that he could teach me some plus points on spirituality. He is very smart looking and about my height. He looks very similar to the available sketch. His persona will remain with me for a long time. Thank you.

REPRESENTING GOLDEN BOOK
23-10-79

This experience took place in the higher planes but below the soul plane and there were three temples made of white marble. In one of the temples, some people represented different religions. I was also there. Some of them were fighting with each other, although they represented religions.

I stood among them but very calm with one book in my hand, very close to my heart.

'Then someone asked me, what are you representing?

I said; I am representing 'The Golden Book.'
The Eternal Truth

LITTLE GOLDEN DEER
29-10-1979

This experience took place on the soul plane. The buildings, land and grass everything was golden. A baby deer was also of golden colour. The baby deer is a symbol of another Soul.

This baby deer was eating golden grass and trotting about and looking at me. I enjoyed it very much as that baby deer was playing near me. I also felt like eating the golden grass. 'So I did.' As they say, the golden scenery was so beautiful, 'out of this world.' This was an experience to teach me, so I can answer back to those who want to know, 'What is spiritual freedom? Once you cross the boundaries of lower planes, you will feel free similar to this little golden deer.

TELEPATHY 'LIVE'
12 noon 31-10- 1979

One day I was walking on Southall Broadway when I heard Mr P. Singh call me. I looked around in all directions but he was not there. Later in the evening, I saw another Seeker,

Mr Darshan Manic, at his house. While we were standing in the entrance hall, this Seeker made a call to Mr P. Singh.

I asked this Seeker to ask Mr P. Singh why he called me in the afternoon. Then Mr P. Singh replied; I wanted to see you, 'Why did you not come? I had acquired this ability to hear people who would think of me.

TELEPATHY 'LIVE'
Morning 2-11-1979

A fellow worker, Mr K. Atwal, was thinking about me while I was working on a printing machine at UK Corrugated. I heard him call me but I could not see him when I looked around. I noted the time; it was 6 am as we worked a night shift that week.

At 6.55 am, I met him in the locker room and asked him if he had any problems. To which he said, No. Then I asked him if he was calling me at 6 am, to which He replied, 'Yes' I was thinking about you around 6 am. He was very sincere to me because I forecasted the birth of his two sons. He was aware of my spiritual abilities.

SADHU 'SAINT'
3-11-1979

One day as I was passing by some Indian-style houses, surprisingly, my aunty appeared in one of them. She greeted me and said to me;

> I had a dream about you, that very soon,
> you will be a Sadhu.

I asked: 'How soon and what kind of Sadhu? She replied, 'Very soon and the type of that you will look like a Hindu gentleman with a bag in your hand.' It was a clear indication for 1981 because our spiritual Masters don't wear any orange colour (Bhagwa-Rang) clothes; we appear as regular gentlemen.

───────────────── ❧❧ ─────────────────

LOWER WORLDS
8-11-1979

This experience is based on a few days when the spiritual Master appeared to me daily on a journey into the astral, causal, mental and etheric planes. The purpose was to familiarise me with all the planes, lords and rulers.

I was shown these planes in full detail, such as the capital of each plane, sounds and colours. Later on, Master asked me to give an introduction talk to some people, explaining the five bodies of a man and how to achieve Self and God-realisation in this life.

FUTURE SPIRITUAL MASTER
15-11-1979

Experience; I am the present spiritual Master and Dapren is with me. But he is standing behind me, watching while I meet and greet people. It was a very short but to the point experience.

CLOAK OF GOD-MAN
17-11-1979

I went to see someone, a 'psychic.' He used an entity to forecast the past, present and future. I saw he was already telling somebody about the future without any problem. When he finished, I asked him if he could tell me about the past and future. He said, 'Yes' as he was about to begin, I focused on the spiritual Master and chanted Haiome. He tried but could not get through.

'Someone asked what the matter was? The psychic replied that he had some kind of guardian angel with him. So,

I cannot tell him anything. Nothing can enter your psychic space when the Master is with you and you are chanting Haiome.

BABA NAND SINGH
23-11-1979

Today, before I went to sleep, I requested the Master to guide me. How to become a good soul traveller and body remover 'Direct projection.' Instead, a saint, my first guru Baba Nand Singh of Nanak-Sar appeared and I was shown his early life. His eyes made lots of impression on me.

His message was, 'Stay in balance.'

It was a clear indication that I was pushing myself beyond limits when there was no need. I said ok.

HEART CHAKRA 'LIVE'
2 pm 26-11-1979

Before going to sleep, I remember that my hand was on the heart area. I had often heard not to place the hands on the chest while sleeping. I wanted to experiment. This time, I left my hand there purposely to see what would happen and what could be done to prevent it. After a few minutes, I fell asleep. The weight of my hand was on the heart area; the body began to relax. The 'Heart Chakra' began to open and so many entities appeared, jumping all over me. They were trying to scare me in every possible way they could.

I got scared initially because that's what they were trying to do. After a while, I opened my eyes but they were still there. I could not move my hand from the heart area because my body had gone numb. So, in the presence of all these entities, I searched my brain with wide-open eyes. Then suddenly, an idea struck my mind to use my legs.

I lifted my right leg, which was not that easy and placed it on top of the left leg and twisted the body over to a sideways position. As I did so, the hand came off the heart area. The heart chakra closed and all of the entities disappeared and once again, I was a free man. I hope this experiment may be helpful to some. That is only possible if you can remember and twist your body to remove your hand from the 'Heart Chakra.'

WORD OF GOD
Night 27-11-1979

Experience; I was in some kind of master-ship selection meeting. There were some people in the hall. There was no one on the stage but somebody would come as a judge. As a competitor, I had a suitcase in my hand which contained;

The word of God

Another competitor had a suitcase in his hand but it contained something else. 'I never asked what?

THE JOURNEY
30-11-1979

This experience is about the journey of the Soul. I am using 'horse' as an example. One day the horse left his house, 'Soul Plane' and wandered around on the roads. Complicated about his long journey, he ran and ran, exhausted. He sees green fields and jumps over the fence as grass always appears greener on the other side but there are more hurdles once crossed over. It was even more complicated and there was some kind of battleground he had to struggle with more than before.

There was a black army 'Negative force' sitting in the trenches to attack the white army 'Positive force.' 'This is the fight within' This horse arrived and he ran through the trenches of the black army and the negative force ran away. Finally, the horse reached the white army that was waiting for him.

A cameraman, 'Seeker,' wanted to photograph the horse but unfortunately, the camera reel finished. Then the Master said to the cameraman, 'You cannot take his photograph; he has gone beyond your range.' The horse was free once more and he returned to his real home, where he belonged. 'Soul Plane'

GOLDEN HAIR
3 am 5-12-1979

Experience; I saw that all of my hair were of a golden colour but I was wondering, 'Why did I dye my hair this colour? It was a clear indication of my present state of consciousness.

HEALER
9-12-1979

I was standing on the stage and I am a spiritual healer. There were so many people to receive healing. As people approached me, I told them, Yes, you will be healed now. Those who came were all healed.

FATHER GOT HEALINGS
10-12-1979

My father suffered from kidney stones for over 15 to 20 years. Doctors had suggested surgery. He was too scared and did not want to follow Doctors' advice. Every time he went to the bathroom to urinate, he made very painful noises.

To be honest, I was getting fed up with his suffering because that bathroom was next to my little room.

I did not want to hear anything because I am in meditation most of my spare time. One day I said to the Master, 'Sort him out Yaar' 'Yaar means friend'; this is how I used to call him most of the time. The next time he went to the bathroom, all his system had cleared up; his pain never returned ever since.

'Thank you, Master'

HEALING FOR A FRIEND
14-12-1979

One day, a friend came to see me and began to cry over my shoulder. When I asked him, 'What is the problem? He told me that one of his uncles, 'Chacha' whom I knew also, had a severe stroke; he was paralysed on one side. He requested if a spiritual Master could help. I also got emotional as I knew the person well. I communicated internally and the answer came positively and within a week, this person was healed completely.

Thank you, Spirit

KAL'S TRAP 'LIVE'
15-12-1979

This is an example: How Kal set up the trap in disguise to mislead you sometimes. Always challenge 'The Entity' if you can. But sometimes, it is not possible because you get so involved with the story and it looks surreal to you. This is my real story.

One day I was working on the machine 'UK Corrugated,' a fellow worker Mr John came to see me and said, 'Do you know that Mr David's wife died? (David is a fellow worker). He said that I went to his house to pay respects when his daughter came into the room and asked her dad, 'Where is my mother? Mr David replied, 'From where shall I get your mummy? She has gone to heaven. After listening to their emotional conversation, John said, 'The tears came out of my eyes.'

I passed this message on to another worker, who also knew Mr David but he said; He was not aware of this sad news. After a few days, I went to Heathrow airport, London and I saw Mr David at the airport, as he was going to America for holidays. But to my surprise, I saw that his wife was with him because I knew her by face. I went to see that fellow worker who made this statement a few days earlier. He replied; 'I never made this statement to you or anyone else.'

Then instantly, I realised that the Kal power had used him as a channel but without knowing that he had been used. So I excused myself from him by saying that it might have been someone else. But I could have created trouble for myself if I had opened my mouth to Mr David.

Be aware of Kal traps.

PAST LIFE
20-12-1979

Experience; Master took me into the past to let me know who I was. During the sixteenth century, I was one of the religious Masters. As several religions were competing with each other at that time. I will not mention my name or religion, as this could upset many people. I don't think it is a wise thing to do. I also don't want people to make any guesses because, as far as I am concerned, it has no value whatsoever, especially to myself.

Past is Past

To my surprise, people still worship my past, although I am not there anymore. It does not bother me at all. The teachings of 'The Way to God' say past Masters have done their duties and gone into the new arena allotted by God.

PAST LIFE
27-12-1979

Master and I went further back in time (silver-age). Nature was in full bloom and the greenery was excellent; the sky was as blue as possible. The weather was very much in the balance. My habitant mainly was jungle. I spent most of my time in meditation and my life span in this life was approximately three thousand years.

The life span of other humans was also a few centuries old. As a human, I was alone in the jungle. Even now, I prefer to stay alone physically as much as possible. Due to my past life in the wilderness, I immensely love animals because they were my companions. Humans have a very short memory; we have been through every life form, so please love them all.

PAST LIFE
28-12-1979

This time, Master and I went back to the times of Mohammad, the prophet of Islam. This was a meaningful life as well. From a physical perspective, this was one of my happiest lives. I was also a camel trader and I was married to a very beautiful lady who always preferred to wear white clothes. We never had any children in that life but we always felt top of the world.

She is also here but as a family friend, she is not aware of this because I have never told her. This is not a wise thing to do and as I have said before, the past is past. We should pay attention to the present life and its responsibilities. She is here to work off her karmas with her current family. I am here to do my duty in another dimension. We must learn to move on and never get stuck with our past; otherwise, we will never move forward. There is only one relation to which you should pay attention to 'That is God!

God was with you in the past; God is with you 'Now' and will be with you in the future. All others are companions, very similar to leaves on the tree. Every year the tree gets new leaves in spring and they all fall off in autumn. This is similar to all human reincarnations. We have new relations at birth and depart from them at our human death.

'So, we make a fresh start every time.'

MORE TRAINING
1-1-1980

Experience: I was busy working and Master came around. When I saw that my Master had come, I approached him and shook hands. While shaking hands, he looked at our hands, both his and mine. I saw that my hands were smaller than his hands. The size of the hands is a symbol. He said; Go back to your work; you have a lot to do. Then I returned to my work and continued. It was clear that I must keep striving toward my spiritual goal.

PAUL & I ARE ONE
9-1-1980

This experience took place in Trumpers Way, Hanwell. The little cross is marked in the sketch. It is a very rough road and there are little hills in the shape of landscapes. I watched Paul ji, as he was walking towards me, while I was standing in the middle of the road. When Paul Ji came near and to my surprise, he physically disappeared.

Then suddenly, I lost my personality too and felt myself walking and being as though I was Paul Ji. It happened like Paul Ji and I merged into one person. So instead of two people, only one person was walking. I was aware of myself and Paul Ji at the same time.

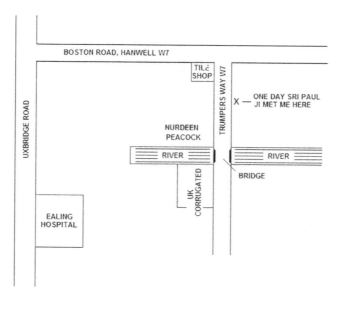

HAIRBREADTH OF DIFFERENCE 'PAUL JI'
16-1-1980

Paul Ji came and took me on a long journey into the inner planes. He said to pay attention to the experience that there is only a hairbreadth of difference between all the planes. This was a long experience; first, we were on the physical plane and then proceeded to the astral plane. Then suddenly, we were on all the planes at the same time. Paul Ji said, now all of your bodies are fully awakened on each plane simultaneously. He said this way you can have experience on all the planes simultaneously.

Later: People were carrying some silver or metal coins in their baskets. When I touched any coin, it turned into a gold coin; people were amazed at this miracle. We had a long and detailed experience on the astral and causal planes. Then he took me to the mental plane and said; this is the mental plane. He said this because I asked him. Although I was aware of it, I don't know why I asked him. Again, it was a long experience on the etheric plane in full detail.

If I remember correctly, I was carrying something golden all the time, either it was a golden coin or a golden ring. While we were on the mental or etheric plane, we always talked about the soul plane. Paul Ji gave me all these experiences because of my upcoming assignment. This was the first-ever when Paul Ji took me on a journey into the inner planes. We had met many times before in different experiences but I do not recall if he ever took me on a spiritual journey, as it had been Dapren all the time.

Thank you - Paul Ji.

PAUL JI'S BOOK
18-1-1980

It was a very long experience within Paul Ji's comic book. I was standing in green fields and there were lots of wild animals. Most of the animals were very friendly to me and I had a 'Comic Book' in my hand. I was going through it, page by page, including the illustrations of Paul and Rebazar Tarz. I was also on every page but doing something of my own.

I was amazed, how come Paul Ji illustrated me on every page of his book, as this book has been written long before I became his Seeker. At the same time, I felt very strongly that Paul Ji had done this so that people would accept me without any hesitation when I became the Master. My conclusion to this experience was that I also had the same experiences that Paul-Ji had. There is no doubt because Dapren has shown me all these planes.

While going through this lengthy experience, Dapren's powerful presence was with me all the time. As I said, I was on every page of this book but not directly with Paul or Rebazar. This simply means that I have been on each plane but that the experiences are slightly different.

GOD-REALISATION
23-1-1980

Experience: I talked to another Seeker, saying; 'I am the next person to be God-realised.' Then I changed the subject. I realised that I should not discuss this with him and said; We all will be God realised soon. The experience stopped and continued later on. Somebody told me that a God-realised person could go up to that level of consciousness within the count of three. It should take that amount of time or you should be dwelling in this state of consciousness.

POLITICS
27-1-1980

Experience; I was having a conversation with Mr P. Singh.
Singh: 'You can use a little bit of politics?
Sher: I don't have any politics.
Singh: Everybody has a bit of politics.
Sher: Not me; I don't have any.
He was surprised that I don't have any politics at all.
He was amazed.
In reality, it is true.
Politicians don't bother me simply because they are not in my line of interest.
I do not vote for anybody.

GURU GOBIND SINGH JI
30-1-1980

Guru Gobind Singh is the last and tenth Guru of Sikhism. He was the Master during the 17th century. He was born on 22 December 1666 and passed away on 21 October 1708. I received some instructions from Guru Gobind Singh that was part of my training. In this experience, I was pretty aware of being the next spiritual Master but that learning was essential.

BODY
14-2-1980

Experience; Suddenly, my vibrations were sky high then I felt that Master was around, although I did not see him. I reassured myself not to worry; it was only him. After that, another body popped up, out of my physical body. It was standing right in front of me but slightly higher in height. It was strange that I looked at my spiritual body from the physical body; instead of the spiritual body looking at the physical body. I was only able to see above knees level and below nose level. I tried to look at the whole body but was not successful.

The first indication: It was not a physical body.
Second: By the Master's grace, your physical body can also see the spiritual body.
In the world of Spirit, everything is possible.

TO SEE GOD IN 5 SECONDS 'LIVE'
19-2-1980

Due to some reasons, I went to see Mr Manic; I sat in the front room alongside his brother on the sofa. Mr Manic talked to another person in the room and said, pointing at me, 'This man can reach a God-realisation state of consciousness within 5 seconds.'

After he said that, I asked him; 'How do you know?

He answered, 'Because Spirit has given me this experience.'

SAI BABA
20-2-1980

Experience: There was a picture (Photo) of Sai Baba; he was born in 1838 and died on 15 October 1918. There was some spiritual meeting. During the experience, someone said; Only those who have the same state of consciousness as

Sai Baba should pick up his photo. I picked up his picture because I was the only person there who had the same state of consciousness.

MONTHLY REPORT 'COPY'
26-2-1980

Dear Master: I have been going through an extraordinary experience now, what I call a mind-less state of consciousness. It appears I don't have any mind at all. The people I come across daily make some remarks and I do not seem to catch the real meaning. I am talking about everyday conversations.

Even when I am driving, I am sitting in the driver's seat, holding the steering wheel, going at a certain speed or in an area of heavy traffic. The car is moving and stopping at junctions and for a long time, I am away 'Soul' from the car in the real sense.

Suddenly I realise, that I am supposed to be driving the car. Then I promise myself that; I will stay alert the next time but the same thing happens repeatedly and every day. The same thing happens when I am operating machinery at work. I am not worried, though I just wonder sometimes, 'Where am I at that time? Thank you for your guidance.

Yours in Spirit

THE ANSWER
27-2-1980

Master leads me to this experience to explain my mind-less state and Souls' control of the physical body. I had a bicycle and walked along with it, steering it in the right direction without any problem. I was dealing with traffic, pedestrians and all my physical body situations. I was somewhere else in my soul body, functioning the same but doing something else with full responsibility.

Then I wondered, 'Where is my bicycle? Then I realised; It was with my physical body. Then I began to search for my physical body carrying the bicycle.

Finally, I found my physical body and at the same time, I merged into my physical body, became one again and carried on with the bicycle. The Master showed me that I could travel anywhere in the soul body but the physical body is being looked after and guided by the Spirit. For almost three continuous years, it was a struggle for me to stay within my physical body.

These days all the Seekers are struggling to do soul travel just once. I am struggling with my soul body to stay within my physical body. I am just wondering, 'What is their problem?

THE LIGHT
5-3-1980

Experience; I have seen the divine light in its pure form. So, you look at everything not as a structure or as trees but as light through your soul body. Where ever I looked, I saw the light everywhere. All the buildings, shops, walls or any kind of physical object turned into light. It was the spectrum at its best. The mixer of all 'lights' shining so beautifully, I enjoyed it. I wish every person could look at the world from this viewpoint.

It was a display of light in pure form; the colours changed according to the structure work. If someone looks with spiritual sight, this is how all the structural work would appear. An atom structure of light blended.

It was a wonderful expression of light in pure form.

BABA BALAK NATH 'LIVE'
7-3-1980

I borrowed two books from a follower of Baba Balak Nath. He appears as a child aged twelve years, although he is approximately 710 years old as a saint. He stays the same age throughout all the years. He still appears to his followers and guides them accordingly because I know some of them.

I read two of his books and at night-time, he appeared live at my sleeping place and physically woke me up. I turned around and saw him standing there. He said to me to have; Darshan.

Darshan means Glimpse

Straight away, I noticed that he was alone. I did not see my Master with him, so I said to myself, 'If he came alone without him, I would not have darshan,' so I turned around and went to sleep. He left the place as well. I don't know if I have done the right or wrong thing but I did not like his coming alone, without the permission of my Master.

MY VILLAGE
8-3-1980

I was in my village in India and some kind of upheaval was coming to destroy everything. The disruption was very colourful in some sort of circles. These circles were moving slowly towards the village from all directions. These circles were very close. This time I raised my hand and said to the village; I bless you in the name of God. Everything stopped and the village was saved. Spirit was demonstrating my ability if I am required to do something.

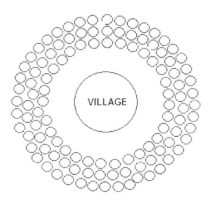

DIRECT PROJECTION
19-3-1980

Today I wanted to practice direct projection. I locked the room and sat in the practice position. First, I did my meditation for 45 minutes to calm all my mind and body tensions.

1. I began my practice and almost straight away, I felt that my Soul was coming out through the spiritual eye and it did. I was concentrating on an area about 5ft in front of my sitting and it was there in no time, after a while, it went back into the body again.

2. I concentrated again and in no time it was out. This time I wanted to go outside; I went through the door and halfway down the stairs when I changed my direction and returned to my body.

3. I concentrated again and went near the window in my soul body. I was still inside the room but my vision was blurred and not very clear. I thought I better open my eyes but instead, my physical eyes opened.

4. I concentrated again in the same area and then my wife came and knocked on the door. The dinner was ready, to which I was not interested anyway but I had no choice; I had to get up physically from my position.

Total time 1.15 pm to 3 pm.

This was not a successful session as I practiced direct projection; instead, the soul body kept popping out. I tried again at 10 pm to sit for meditation first, then I concentrated on direct projection but I landed in one of the higher planes through the third eye. Instead of my practice of direct projection, my soul body let me down every time; as I said earlier, this was my problem, it would not stay within.

PARA-VIDYA
4-4-1980

Experience; I was dealing with carpenters and some other workers. It was my afternoon shift; before that, I went to see Dapren as he was in England. During the day, I wondered if I could ask Master to read my para-vidya for my past and future. I met him in the hallway for a few minutes. Then an idea came into my mind to see him in private. I approached him and asked him, 'For how long will you stay in England?

He knew why I was asking him; instead of telling me for how long, he began to say to me what I had been doing during the daytime. Then he said, 'Why do you want to know these things? He was hinting at the para-vidya reading. He said; You are one of the most advanced students and you know that. I knew what he meant because I already knew my future. Sometimes there is some curiosity sitting in one corner of your mind.

PARA-VIDYA 'ALL NIGHT'
8-4-1980

Yesterday I was reading the para-vidya book and at night-time, training begins, it lasted all night. I finished my meditation at 12.35 am 'night,' and the training was between 12.35 am to 7 am. This was a continuous experience, all based on para-vidya. To be honest, I did not understand a bit about it physically. I could remember the experience or training given to the soul body directly.

I am not a sound sleeper; I must have woken up at least ten times in that period. All I could remember was that my experience stopped and continued again from the same point as I fell asleep again. All the sacred numbers were;

1-3-5-6-7-8-9-10-11-12-20

They kept repeating in my memory. I felt like I was a computer but somebody else was doing the programming.

74

Number 3 was visible at times and number 20 repeated quite often; I am sure there must be some special reason for these particular numbers. 'We wait and see?

SPIRIT
9-6-1980

I was told a lucky spot in my house, 'I don't know where? During the experience, there was a scene and a waterfall took place in a giant fish tank. I do have a fish tank but it is only 32 gallons capacity. I was standing under this waterfall. There was a golden plate on one side and a silver plate underneath and nectar was dropping into it. The plates were removed and I don't know to whom the golden plate was given but the silver plate was given to me and I was told that Spirit has special connections with me.

GUARDIAN ANGEL
30-6-1980

I was passing by some fields and saw a snake and by mistake, I threw a stone at him and he ran away. After that, some other hostile forces began to fight with me; I defended myself and fought back. A guardian angel intervened and told the negative forces to leave me alone and they stopped. I was shown that I have the protection and my guardian angel.

SOUL PLANE
1-7-1980

I was called upon and two invisible angels came to collect me. They took me to the soul plane where Master was waiting but when I reached there;

Master said; Not him; he is already here.

Then the angels brought me back. I think the angels were supposed to take someone else or that the experience was trying to tell me that I am already established here.

COINS OF GOLD
2-7-1980

Master and I were together, he had a sack of golden coins and they were shining brilliantly as they had just been freshly made for me. He gave me two hands full of coins. We visited my father during the same experience, who was in India; he was also holding similar golden coins. He also gave them to me.

NEW MAN 'MYSELF'
3-7-1980

I was wearing a red tracksuit. Master asked me to take it off. He offered a better and large blue tracksuit that fitted my body very well; I became a spiritual man. By letting me know, Master created a test with the assistance of Maya-Illusion. There was a lady who was a channel for the negative power. She was playing all kinds of tricks on me. Being a spiritual man, I knew that she was an Illusion; I did not respond to her but let it be.

Since that day, I have been feeling much better again spiritually because I had a downtime recently. It was due to very intense spiritual training.

'Thank you, Master'

MYSTERIOUS
5-7-1980

I was lying down and just thinking about Spirit; I had a short nap, 'half-sleep,' during that time. When I woke up, I opened my eyes and wanted to do some video recording at 11.55 am for children. But next to me, I saw 'something' moving; I began to get up into the sitting position, at the same time that 'Something' also started to get up into the sitting position and it was about two feet away from my face.

I went again into the original lying-down position as you would usually sleep in. The presence was powerful. As I moved, it also moved; then I thought to feel it with my hands. Instead, I decided to turn my face in that direction. I slowly turned around and I saw very similar looks to me lying right in front of me. It was my soul body lying next to me all the time and now we were looking at each other.

I was aware of both sides or bodies.

HIGHER INITIATIONS
6-7-1980

Experience; I was in our Satsang class and discussed the topic of Initiations. One of our members asked about my initiations; I am unsure if he said I had only the fifth initiation. I said that this was not true; I also had higher initiations.

SATSANG
7-7-1980

We were about to attend Satsang with Dapren. About 20 people were in the small hall, including Mr Manic and Tarzan. I was outside the hall waiting for the Master and I saw him coming. In my feelings, I usually sit at the back of the Satsang class, so I did. But on that day, 'I don't know how? Although I placed myself at the back, I found myself sitting in the front row.

Today In our Satsang, we were discussing, 'What is reality? During Satsang, one of our members was talking about something else. Master said; 'Shall we discuss reality today? It was shown that some members are attending the Satsang but their minds are somewhere else.

I woke up physically.

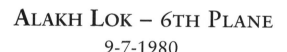

ALAKH LOK – 6TH PLANE
9-7-1980

I went to bed at midnight. I was still awake, Dapren appeared and said; We have seen lots of colours and we have seen enough gold; now it is about time, we should go into the silver colours. I knew Master was talking about going beyond the soul plane. As soon as he said that, my vibrations were sky-high within my forehead.

We applied soul travel and landed in Alakh Lok; The place looked very familiar; the Soul was or is in an actual state of beingness, be yourself and let the others be.

ALAYA LOK – 7TH PLANE
13-7-1980

I had lots of interest in this plane being the seventh, Baba Isher Singh mentioned this plane quite often to his followers. **'Assi bhai sat walait 'Britain' de malik haa'** (Punjabi). The conclusion was that he could travel up to the seventh plane any time he felt like it. Later I came to know that he had gone beyond that.

Mohammad also mentioned the seven heavens. So It was essential for me to explore this plane. One day I received a pamphlet in which it was written; Truth is never denied of a man if he asks in his heart. One day I requested Dapren if he could show me the truth.

One night Master came and said; Let us explore the truth today. In no time, we both landed in Alaya Lok. He mentioned this is the seventh plane and of truth. The journey or exploration was long, as Alaya Lok is vast in size. What I have seen up here is different from the lower world. It is complicated to write in words. In simple terms, it is the plane of bliss state of consciousness. You do not want to leave but the Master nodded, 'Let us go; there is much more to explore yet and higher.'

Indeed, it was the plane of truth.

HAKIKAT LOK – 8TH PLANE
19-7-1980

Hakikat Lok is the next realisation; Hakikat Purukh is in-charge of this plane. Dapren introduced me to this lord and he showed me around for a long time. This plane is beyond time but I compared being a physical man. After having this long experience and being anxious, I wanted to go to the next plane. Master said, 'No, we are staying here for tonight; we will make a move in the morning.'

I said, ok. There is no such thing as the night on this plane. Again, it was a physical expression because I was so anxious to explore all the planes in one go. Master indicated, don't rush; once your learning is finished here, we will make a move. I said ok, thank you. In this plane, it is everlasting brilliance beyond description. This Hakikat-realisation is mentioned in the Guru Granth of Sikhism. I felt that I am one of the most privileged person to have this realisation.

RESIDENCE OF MASTER 'LIVE'
27-7-1980

One day I was standing in our bedroom upstairs and looking through the window; I saw Dapren coming inside the house. Then I received the message by telepathy that Master lived in this house; Then, he went inside his room.

Short but an awe-inspiring experience

EUROPEAN SEMINAR - 31-7-1980
Bern, Switzerland: 8, 9, 10 August 1980

I had an experience just before the European Seminar and I might be asked to go on stage to give a talk on higher planes. First, I thought of writing some notes to prepare myself if I got called on the stage. But then I decided not to do it; I will deal with it when the time comes. I felt confident that I should not have any problem explaining it. So, I went to the seminar in Switzerland. I had very high vibrations throughout the journey, at the seminar and on the way back. We travelled by coaches.

I felt like a God realised soul.

He did not call me on the stage; 'Dapren waved at me' while he talked, indicating that I would be dwelling in God's state of consciousness. Once the talk finished, Dapren and I managed to have a short meeting, during which he gave me a clear hint about the next step and a photograph was taken outside afterwards.

I was an example to the others for my peaceful and positive attitude. At the same time, others were blowing their tops off due to the rough journey and faulty coaches. Lots of time was wasted on coach repair work and later taking the wrong route. We ended up in Luxemburg. Most of us did not have the visa to be in that country. We gave our honest explanation of how it all happened; they let us through. Our area In-charge Mrs N. Tember noticed my positive attitude and asked me if I could write something for the 'Voice of Eck' which I did.

Later; I was not very happy when I read the Voice of Eck because the editor added something I never said.

AGAM LOK – 9TH PLANE
3-1-1981

Dapren prepared our journey and we landed in Agam Lok. This is where you will have the total experience of Soul enlightenment. I felt this is my peak time. I felt like the picture of purity. I was like a mirror, reflecting the Spirit of God all the time and I said to myself, 'Yes, I have done it.' I strongly felt that I am a unit of God's awareness in the true sense. I have achieved God-realisation.

I achieved nothing but only became aware of what I already had. I could hear the sound everywhere. Then suddenly, it came very close to my ears; when I settled, I could hear the sound of Woodwinds, very melodic and in the whole rhythm.

GOD REALISATION
10-1-1981

Dapren came as usual in his soul body and due to some reasons, my vibrations were a lot higher than expected. He said; I have got something to give you. He asked me to put forward both my hands. He had written No.8 on a piece of paper and No.9 on another paper.

First, he put No. 8 in my hands; saying, this is your 8th initiation due from last time and then he put No. 9 in my hands. I was pleased.

Then I asked him, 'Does this mean God's realisation? He said, Yes.

Then he explained that these initiations are significant, especially the ninth; You have just entered the line of Vairaagy Masters.

CONCERT
5-3-1981

Later, on 5th March 1981, Dapren came to London to have a Music Concert at Westminster. His biography 'Heaven to Prairie' was available at the concert. We had a handshake and he signed this book for me. It is very well written and it is so uplifting. I felt I could not put it down until I finished.

He clarifies the point of receiving his 9th initiation when Sri Paul Ji prepared his entry in the line of Vairaagy Masters.

PRIOR TO WORLDWIDE
2-4-1981

I am getting the information in many ways, as time is approaching close to the worldwide seminar. I was told what kind of clothes I was supposed to buy. I was told to buy a light blue colour suit. I have been guided to get a USA visa for travelling purposes. Which I did and I received so much more information.

I felt that this is my peak time for staying in purity; I am like a mirror, reflecting Spirit or God and nothing else. I feel, 'Yes, I have made it' towards my 'Destiny,' for which I have waited for years. I am getting many more experiences regarding more or higher initiations. I cannot write anything at present as I have a very short time writing and preparing myself. So the majority of the experiences are slipping through my fingers unrecorded. As a reminder, there is too much repetition of similar experiences.

SPIRITUAL NAME
9-4-81

After the Ninth initiation, I asked Spirit if I could know my spiritual name. Very similar to Padder Zaskq and Dapren. I was told, Your name is;

'AVTAR'

Later, when I was travelling with Master, everyone called me by this name on all the planes. **Avtar.**

MASTER-SHIP
4-7-1981

I had a minor but awe-inspiring experience in which I was told that my area In-charge, Mr P. Singh, had been informed spiritually that I would be the next spiritual Master.

IKK-SAR
Thursday 16-7-1981

As I said recently, many experiences had gone unrecorded regarding the 10th and 11th initiation. I felt that writing about these experiences was not as important as moving forward with my mission of a lifetime. Today Dapren appeared again as usual; without wasting any time, he asked me to form a lap using both of my hands. This is your position at present. He said again, '**This is your 12ᵗʰ initiation**' and he put this piece of paper No. 12 in my hands and we both shook hands.

'I said thank you, Master'

I felt so down to earth and very grateful to the Master.

MY TALK
3-8-1981

I thought all day, 'What am I going to say at the seminar and how will I begin my talk? Because I am a very shy person. I don't think many people are aware of this. To give me confidence, Master created the experience.

There was a big hall very similar to the spiritual seminar; many Seekers were in the hall. I was going to give a talk. I continuously talked about God's teaching from 8 am to 8 pm for 12 hours. Master was listening too in this meeting. During the talk, I made precious points. People were pleased. After my talk, I sat near Dapren's chair and he looked at me.

He said, well, you can talk for days on this subject.
Sher; Yes, I can talk all my life.'

HAIOME CHANTS
From 1978 to 1981

I attended the spiritual chants regularly in our respective area, Slough. The problem I am facing is, staying conscious throughout the 30 minutes. Every time I sang Haiome a few times, the spiritual experience would begin.

I tried very hard to stay conscious but could not, although I never purposely wanted to have any experience. But I could not help it. I counted up to twelve experiences in thirty minutes and all of them were on different subjects. After chanting the Haiome a few times, my soul body clicked out. My soul did not want to stay within my physical body. As I said before, this had been my problem all along.

BABA BUDAH JI
5-8-1981

Baba Budah Ji is mainly related to Sikhism, 'Budah' means very old. At a very young age, he met Guru Nanak. During their conversation, Guru Nanak was so impressed after listening to this child he said to him: Although you are so young, you speak like an older man. This means a sage person because this child was born with a spiritual awakening. Since then, he was given the nickname Baba Budah Ji.

He assisted six gurus in accepting master-ship. Each time, he was the person to do all the preparations for this ritual. He also forecasted the birth of the sixth Guru in line, Sri Hargobind sahib. He said; this boy would be a saint and a warrior upon giving the forecast. He was also appointed as a tutor by fifth guru Arjan dev.

He was born on 6 October 1506 and died on 8 September 1631. That makes him 125 years old. When Guru Arjan Dev assembled the Guru Granth Sahib, the holy book of Sikhism, Baba Budah Ji was appointed the first priest to read it.

Dapren showed this experience as he was with me and other people were present. I had a container in my hands. There was some Amrit 'Nectar' in this container. People were watching me as I was drinking it. Someone from the crowd said, 'Do you know that is the Amrit from Baba Budah Ji?

So, I take this as a hint of ritual before pass-over, 'The spiritual mantle' by Dapren.

ANAMI LOK
9-10-1981

Anami means 'Name-less' or something that is beyond description. I was within my small box room, where I meditated for most of my time. I was woken up; I saw nine people standing around me. Although the room was so small but at that moment, it opened up like anything, so there was no shortage of space. At that time, I realised that they are the 'Nine super Souls' from God. These are the people who are very near to God and they take commands directly from God.

We were travelling and in no time, we were on this plane; I felt as though I was in the presence of God. I was told; Now you are on Anami lok. We will perform a spiritual ritual, which is very important before you receive 'The spiritual mantle' from Dapren. I was help-less in comparison to these spiritual giants. All I could do was nod, meaning, **Yes**. They said; this is the final cleansing of your soul body. Although I could not see them, their presence was such, I knew that I was standing in the middle.

No Soul can see each other on this plane as we do on the physical plane. Even Soul loses its appearance; your communication is all within. Once I knew what I was going through, I felt like I was lying on my back in no time. As we do in bed, the bed's purpose was provided by Spirit this time. I was lying but floating on Spirit. I could feel the hands of **Super Souls** dismantling my Soul. I feel a strange but special sensation that you have never felt before. It is a very warm and pleasant feeling.

There was no pain or pleasure during this process but there was happiness as being a unit of God-awareness. You are fully aware of what is taking place and I could sense all the atoms, 'micro size brilliant stars' of my soul body floating about. Once they were satisfied, these **Super Souls** re-assembled my soul body by putting all the stars together as they were original. I felt whole again and stood on my feet, to the effect.

Finally, they brought me back to my little room, where they had initially picked me up. After that, they must have moved to the next mission because they are always on the move. I felt very blessed in their presence and very thankful that they and God had chosen me for this purpose.

'I said, thank you'

Dapren was not with Super Souls during this experience. After that, he did not appear to me during meditation or dreams and his presence was not as strong as it used to be. No further guidance was received from him regarding my travel to the USA or whatever other business. From that day, everything went silent; 'I was wondering why?

On 22ⁿᵈ October 1981, I waited for his appearance up to the last minute but he never came. When the time was up, I said; Baraka Bashad; which Means may the blessings be. **Later**: I heard of the significant change and I said to myself, **'So be it'** I must admit, Yes, I was upset.

NEW MASTER. WORLDWIDE 1981
Letter to Dapren 7-11-1981 **Copy**

Respected Master: I am unfortunate. Life in the future does not look very bright. As you know, I have been under your training for master-ship. I have done my best. I followed your guidance right up to the last minute. I prepared my clothes and I did not sleep all night. My wishes have been left disappointed. On 25-10-1981, my area Mahdi Mr P. Singh rang me and said we had a new spiritual Master.

Well, I am not sad because Mr H...... became the Master. 'I wish him all the luck,' but I have been following your guidance for the same thing. I have received all the initiations and according to your instructions, I have arranged for the U.S.A. visa or whatever relevant preparations I was told to do. I was taken by the 'Nine Super Souls' to Anami-Lok on 9 October 1981 for the final preparation before receiving the spiritual mantle.

But strange enough, from 10ᵗʰ October onwards I have not heard much from you. 'I was wondering why? I thought maybe everything was arranged, so there was nothing more to show or discuss. I was not asked to buy an air ticket or other means of travelling to the U.S.A. I waited for your instructions but I heard nothing. Then I assumed it would be a spiritual lift, similar to when 'Nine Super Souls' came and took me to Anami-Lok.

As I know the result, will I get any favourable position as soon as possible according to my earnings or 'Is it all void now? I did not want to put these words on a piece of paper but now I had to. To make myself clear, where do I stand at the present moment. I am going to India for nine weeks' holidays from 8-11-1981 to 5-1-1982. It would be very kind of you if you could kindly reply to my letter. You may send a letter while I am in India or U.K. I will write down the address of both countries. Address in India .... & .... Address in UK

Yours in Spirit; Sher Gill

MAN IN WAITING 'INDIA'

I waited for a reply from the Master every day via letter or in the dream state but nothing came through. I became upset because of what I was dreaming of and what had happened, looking into the past. So after some time, I decided to step aside from all my spiritual duties.

But I never thought of leaving Spirit because I know from my experience that without Spirit, my life would be dull. I came back to England on 6-1-1982 and checked all the mail during my holidays in India; there was nothing from the Master. So, after a week, I went to see my area Mahdi and told him that I was stepping aside from my duties. I was regularly taking two meetings and Satsang and other responsibilities.

Our area in-charge Mr P. Singh is a very lovely and down to earth person as we have worked as a team in our area. He asked for my reasons but I refused to tell him anything. 'How could I? That was my private world. I never discussed it with anyone because I always believed that you never utter a single word until it all materialises in the physical. Spirit has taught me how to keep my golden silence.

THE BIG ANSWER
2-2-1982

I got the answer from Dapren in a dream state. The experience began in this manner. Two Seekers and I were with him on Southall Broadway. After some talk, Master wanted to go. I told the other Seekers that they could go and I wanted to walk with him to the railway station. So, they left.

Dapren and I were on our way to the railway station; then I asked him, what happened on 22nd October 1981. 'Why did I not get the master-ship? I also told him a number of my experiences that he gave me regarding the master-ship. Then he replied; I never said that you would get the master-ship this time, so everything was clear. It may happen sometime in the future; he gave me a hint;

Paul and I are training you for 1986, I said o.k. Thanks.

Finally, he said; Keep your discipline and carry on taking the two meetings and the Satsang.

Conclusion: I have taken the answer gracefully because you cannot argue with your Master or I was not in the position to argue anyway. As far as I am concerned, this is an evasive answer or to cover up something. The spiritual Master had been guiding me up to 10th October 1981 and 'Super Souls' took me to Anami Lok. Physical Master can make mistakes but 'Super Souls' don't and especially since I was told to get my U.S.A. visa, all the statements and guidance don't add up.

I am sure that something had taken place on the physical, which should not have. It seemed like Dapren had ignored the Spirit. 'What the result be? Time will tell. I cannot utter a single word to anyone; I know people will laugh at me. I have decided to suffer alone, stay silent and move on with my life. At least his last statement regarding 1986 had given me some hope to look forward to. It is not far away; let us wait and see.

GOD-MAN 30-3-1982

Since 22-10-1981, this experience has brought some hope in life. According to what Master had said last time; Paul and I are training you for 1986. According to Paul's statement that the next God-Man (Ma---ta) is fifteen years away, that also means 1986. There was a message displayed on the big board which said;

'God-Man Trial'

After I read this message on the big board an experience began in which I observed many things and situations, such as people with problems and what people had in their minds. Most people were in the traps of Kal. Most of them had lust in their minds. While passing through the village, I observed many people crying over the dead ones. There were dead bodies everywhere; further along, I noticed groups of sad-looking people mourning the dead. I just passed through them, knowing their grief but not being affected by it.

There were many similar situations and I seemed to be within them just at the right time. During this, I woke up and the experience continued while I was fully awake and when I fell asleep again, the experience continued. What I learned through this experience is that 'God-Man' is the true and only representative of God. That is why he is everywhere, knowing, observing, understanding, helping and guiding.

TAKING OVER
Night 3-4-1982

This experience took place in our village, where I saw Dapren as the living Master and was doing all of his duties. I remembered from a conversation that he was a wrestler but he gave it up due to his bad back. I took over all the responsibilities that he used to do.

'This is an indication for the future.'

VISIT OF PAUL AND DAPREN
Night 16-5-1982

This experience took place in our village in India. Paul and Dapren came together to see me. They were with me in our house for 4 to 5 hours. I hoped they might give me good news as they had come together simultaneously. I felt that Dapren is ok physically but Paul had translated from this world and that he must have manifested in a physical body because he was coming with Dapren to see me.

❦

Visit of Satnam Ji
7-10-1982

A year had passed and despite having tremendous knowledge, many doubts began to appear in my mind; 'How could it happen on this path? I was not feeling well spiritually. I thought I was wasting my time in this world. I wondered if Master was aware of anything but I was very disappointed. The question arose in my mind what guarantee is there to materialise in 1986 as Dapren said.

What a waste of life, as I am so fed up nowadays.
'Then Satnam Ji came to revive the life in me.'

I was shown this experience about myself. I saw myself as a boy or young man 'Sher Gill' was sent as a messenger on this earth by this great spiritual being 'Satnam Ji.' But the negative power has caught him and did something nasty to him. It was regarding October 1981. The matter was reported back to this **'Being'** giant living in his world, **'Soul Plane'** beyond description. This spiritual giant appeared in this physical world to investigate. First, I could not see him clearly and then he appeared as a bronze colour; the closest description would be like a negative print or film.

Then he said; I had to take a physical form and investigate.

'What has happened to my Son'
'Exact words said by Satnam Ji'

As soon as he said that, the experience changed from semi-sleep to an awake state. Then he appeared in full form, more or less naked body, bald head and physical body like red Indians. It was Satnam Ji as I have met him before many times. That was an instant spiritual revival. Now I know if Satnam Ji is concerned about my well-being, something will materialise in the future. After our formal meeting, he transformed himself from a physical to beingness state, which means going back to the soul plane.

'Thank you Satnam Ji'

I am the son of such a spiritual giant to which
no one else can claim.

MONTHLY REPORT
10.05 pm. 31-10-1982

Respected Master: I would like to write this letter to thank you for your endless love, which you have showered on me over the past few years up to the present time. The experiences you gave me were wonderful. You have shown me the places in such a short time; I am amazed. I have been thinking of writing a letter to you for the last few days.

I know I have not been very patient but you have been very patient with me. You were nudging, guiding and showing me the way, right from the physical to the highest planes. You are the best companion I have; all other relations are an illusion or maybe some karma to work off here and there, nothing else. Your presence had been with me all the time. I am grateful,

Yours to mould

I have been writing my report every month despite being so close to him to keep my physical side of the discipline. This is one of the copies recorded in my hand written diary.

SEDONA ARIZONA
5 October 1982

Once more, I was surprised to learn what had taken place in Sedona, Arizona, known to be the spiritual city for this path. We probably do need such a place. Dapren, the new Master and a group of Seekers attended a ceremony to establish the seat of power for the ancient teachings. Two flags were displayed in the air; One flag was of the U.S.A. and the other had our E....... symbol. I am shocked by the actions of these two Masters.

I cannot understand what the U.S.A. flag had to do with this ancient teaching. 'Are they trying to turn this teaching into a more physical, political than a spiritual path? I only hope that they know what they are doing. It seems like another decision taking place on the physical, very similar to what had taken place in October 1981. I wonder if they consult the Spirit before making any decision.

Comment: If they carry on doing everything on the physical level, I don't think that there will be much Spirit left within this path. All I can say now is that the results will not be very fruitful unless 'Spirit' is consulted before any action is taken in the future. Only time will tell.

FUTURE 1986
Morning 26-12-1982

This experience took place early in the morning; it was mentioned and written in misty figures, the year will be 1986. I was guided to concentrate on Spirit as much as possible in the meantime.

GUIDANCE FROM PAUL JI
Monday 10.30 pm 27-12-1982

Experience; I was made aware today that Paul Ji will guide me for the training of God-Man from now onwards and concentrate on Paul Ji's guidance during meditation and moment to moment.

'I am grateful.'

GOD ON LINE
Night 30-1-1983

I came out of our house at 43 Leamington Road, Southall, to do something for someone. Suddenly, somebody called me from behind as I walked towards Tachbrook Road. She had a telephone receiver in her hand and she said to me; Here is your telephone.

'IT's God... It's from God'

I said I would be back in a minute, so I went. When I came back, somebody gave me a message from God. 'You are the next spiritual Master.'

A JOGY 'SAGE'
2-2-1983

During this experience, I was on a farm in India in my village. There were some people with me. Maybe in his sixties, a middle-aged man came; he appeared as an enlightened Soul. He said he had seen me within his spiritual eye and knew that I was a saint. He wanted to touch my feet, 'an Indian custom to receive blessings,' but I did not allow him. I moved backwards but on his behalf, other people requested to let him do that. He touched my feet and felt blessed.

GOD PROMISE
Wednesday Night 13 April 1983

Experience; There were several people and a chosen leader too. There was some dissatisfaction within the group, then somebody said, 'Change him and give the leadership to someone else.' Then somebody else said, 'Who?

Standing among them, I felt great feelings, saying; 'That God has promised me' but I did not utter a single word.

'It made me wonder if something is going
on within Ec..... Organisation'.

———————— ❧ ❧ ————————

SUPER SOULS
2.30 am 17-5-1983

There was some kind of occasion and a group of nine people formed a circle around me and then turn by turn they all expressed their good points. I listened to their points very sincerely. It was all about 'The Way to God.' After the experience, I felt that they were the 'Super Souls' responsible to God.

'Blessed'

———————— ❧ ❧ ————————

NEXT GOD-MAN
18-8-1983

Experience: Dapren was asking, 'Who is the God-Man? There were several Masters. One Master said, **I am** and when he tried to pronounce **God-Man**. He tried many times but failed to pronounce it correctly.

Then again, he asked, 'Who is the next God-Man? I knew that I was but I had promised myself not to utter a word. So, I kept quiet and nobody else claimed, 'That they are.'

GOD-MAN
16-9-1983

Experience: I was with another Seeker and a saint Isher Singh of Nanak Sar. Baba Isher Singh and I were sitting next to each other against the wall and this Seeker was sitting in front of us. Seeker said, pointing at me, 'You are the next God-Man.' I kept quiet and looked at him. I wanted him not to tell anyone what he knew.

In this experience and on the physical, I knew that he had been given the experience. Then Baba Isher Singh moved to one side. Baba Nath, who used to look after me at Nanak Sar, came near to us and we both told the Seeker; if any experience is given to you, try to keep it to yourself. During this experience, I felt baba Ji has connections with the ancient teachings.

DAPREN & BRAHAM
Night 4-10-1983

A group of people were in our house in India and they were making their way towards Dapren, who was sitting and drinking tea in the nearby café. I went ahead and warned him about them; we decided to move from there. Dapren used a spiritual yardstick during the talk and said that all religions finish here. But we are moving ahead of that time. He made a point by saying that most people don't bother to move ahead.

They can move forward but they are stuck in their religions. The spiritual Master came to see me after a long time; he told me all the good things as we walked. As soon as he went, Braham Ji came, whom I had never seen before, on the physical. His picture appears in Paul Ji's comic book. He is working on the mental plane. He looks middle-aged and has a beard about 4 to 5 inches long. He also has long hair that turns grey and is of medium build.

Braham Ji said; I know that Dapren came to see you. Then I said; 'Have they given you any experience about me? Braham Ji said, '**No.**' He added; I know they are again thinking about you. I know what he was trying to say, future spiritual Master.

Comment: Now the bad results are appearing. As I mentioned earlier, an evasive answer was given to me. '**Now**' only time will tell. It was a decision taken on the physical by the Master. Due to whatever reasons, like saying, 'I am the boss.' Spirit backed his decision and a new man became the

Master. As far as I am concerned; 'So be it' If Paul Ji's life span had not been cut short, the history of this path would have been different.

REBAZAR TARZ
Morning 5-12-1983

Although we have met before on many occasions, this is the first time ever that Rebazar appeared to me physically, meaning in the flesh. He has short-cropped hair, a closely trimmed beard, a staff in his hand and wears a robe, the exact description given by Paul Ji in his writings. I especially noted his bottom lip; there is a little line or wrinkle in the centre.

After greeting each other, I walked behind him out of respect. Then we sat down for a while face to face and discussed the subject of God-Man. He is the responsible person for overseeing the passing of the spiritual mantle. He was telling me to prepare myself for this change. I said; 'How much longer do I have to wait? Exact words.

Rebazar; Your time is in 2 years; your turn is coming, Exact words.

I said, '**OK, Sir**' as soon as I said that, he walked away and I stood there watching him go.

'Thank You'

MASTER-SHIP CHANGED
9-1-1984

Today, 9-1-1984 there was a meeting among known spiritual Masters with their blessings. I was also there. Discussion; That the master-ship is changing again. It has been taken back from the new man.

'I asked; 'Why?

A concise answer came,
'Spirit is not very happy with him,' I nodded; Ok.

'I asked: 'Who is next?

It will be given back to Dapren on 12-1-1984. The way Spirit approached to give me this information, I thought, It may be myself. You are next in line, I was told.

Comment: It does not matter what has happened to me but I wish these two gentlemen could come to some mutual agreement for the sake of this Path.

PAUL JI
23-3-1984 Morning 8.00 to 10.45 am

I was thinking of Paul Ji today. During meditation, Paul Ji appeared. He gave me abundant valuable information to prepare me to become God-Man. As we became very friendly with each other, in a very humorous way, 'I asked him?

Sher; 'When will you hand over your spiritual mantle to me?

Paul ji: I am ready now; he pointed at me and said; 'You can have it now if you want to' (Exact words)

Paul Ji; When it is given to you, you must be able to stay above the physical and remain in that state of consciousness all the time.

I said; **Yes, Sir.**

PAUL JI
23-3-1984

In the afternoon of the same day, Paul Ji held a class of about 20 people. I went there. There was a unique book in my hand and I was standing a few yards away from the class. I heard Paul Ji say to the students, pointing at me, 'He has been through it before.' I was pleased about the remarks Paul had made about me.

NEUTRAL 'NOWADAYS'

Nowadays, Paul Ji is training me most of the time. At the same time, I am staying neutral regarding Dapren and the new Man. I believe that they had created this physical mess and both are responsible for it. So let them sort it out between them. I am not interfering or taking sides. I leave it in the hands of Spirit.

THE FEES
Night 22-4-1984

I know that the power is given back to Dapren; still, I was not sending the fee, as I was fed up with him. I had the attitude of, 'Who cares? During meditation, he appeared and said, 'You must send your membership fees because you are next in line.' It was a concise and to-the-point experience.

TWO ROBES
Night 23-4-1984

I was within the golden temple and there was a book. Someone was reading this golden book; He was wearing white clothes. I saw two sets of clothes placed on the marble steps in front of this book. I picked them up separately by their look and scent; I identified these as one belonging to Rebazar Tarz and the other to Dapren.

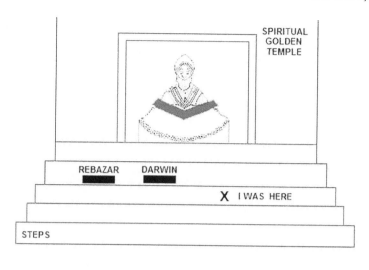

WIND OF CHANGE
Night 27-4-1984

I was inside my house. There were a group of people outside. This was regarding the downfall of this path. One of them represented these people and said to me; you told us to work for this path, we are doing it and now you have gone silent. Due to the current situation, I had been in a neutral position. I came out and made the speech by saying;

This is the path of Enlightenment
Everyone cheered with joy.

Then suddenly, a hefty wind blew. Nobody could hear a thing other than the wind. In the meantime, many people went away and only a few were left. When the wind stopped,

I finished the speech by saying; go back to your communities, do the best you can and don't strain yourself. Take it easy.

May the blessings be.
I felt as if I was Paul Ji speaking.

Comment: This experience showed that many people left and only a few were with Dapren. Those gone are with the new man; there is no need to compare anybody; it is an Individual path and choice.

TAKING OVER AGAIN
Night 28-4-1984

During this experience, I was given practical knowledge about the present situation. Spiritual Master showed me how it all happened practically. I acted out the part of the new man. I held the **spiritual mantle** and Master was watching how I was doing. I had to hold it to make it for at least two years but it slipped away. It was just two years and I lay down and saw the Spirit move out of me and enter Dapren's body.

Comment: Only Spirit knows. 'What the truth is?

FUTURE DELAYED
Saturday Night 16-6-1984

During this experience, I was on the stage and giving a speech about our teachings, being in the position of present spiritual Master. I talked about this path's practical work and said I like doing everything practically. The para-vidya opened up. I was told why the new man had been made the Master. I was told that my training as a God-Man was not yet complete. So, Spirit had accepted him as the stopgap Master at the request of Dapren, due to his poor physical health.

The planning of Spirit was to represent me as the 'God-Man' but not as the living Master. I only managed to clear the 12th Initiation at that time but the requirement is at least 14 initiations. I was also told, That God-Man training could not be accelerated and everything had to be learned the right way around.

Present Comment: I said; Thank you very much. I know what I have learned over 30 years of silence, 'How to keep my mouth shut.' Sometimes I felt like it was a big joke. I don't know how bad was 'Daprens' health, so he decided to give up in 1981. He managed to hold on to his master-ship from 1984 till 2008, which is 24 years. During this period again, he failed to pass this master-ship over to me physically. You can draw your conclusions.

DECISION
17-8-1984

I knew from 9-1-1984 that the spiritual mantle has been given back to Dapren on 12-1-1984. I lingered on not sending the membership fee to either party because I had been in a neutral position for a while. Although I have a life membership with Ec.... Organisation but I discarded that long ago.

A good friend of mine, Mr P. Singh, has done me the honour of writing to the new man that Mr Sher Gill is not our follower anymore. He was the area In-charge at that time; at least he was honest with me for telling the truth. In return, I said to him, Thank You, No hard feelings whatsoever.

Today I have made up my mind on 17-8-1984 to send the membership fee to Dapren. I went to the bank and prepared I.M.O. and posted it. On the same night, during meditation, three Masters appeared. It was Rebazar Tarz and another two; I don't know which one, out of the three spoke or were all three together, who said;

'We thought you might never send it' (Exact words)

All three were very happy to see me do this. All these Masters were aware that no one could take me on a ride as they pleased. I could be stubborn at times. I know I am the son of Satnam Ji and I have been specially sent for this mission. I don't owe anything to either or all of them. I am not begging for master-ship as I have held this spiritual power, God knows how many times. It may be a big thing to them, as far as I am concerned, 'Who cares.'

TOGETHERNESS
13-9-1984

In this experience, It was shown that there would be togetherness. I wish this should occur soon because I feel there are many of our Seekers whose spiritual progress is at a standstill. I am sure that they are not aware of this yet.

'This should happen for the good of the whole.'

INVASION FROM ANOTHER PLANET
Morning 21-10-1984

There were lots of people and they were from another planet. It was a kind of invasion on the physical plane. They had special weapons to wipe out the people. They had some kind of spray; once they sprayed on a person, the person just vanished into thin air. We had to be very careful because you could not tell the difference between them and us except through their actions. I escaped many times, we had a big fight and I was helping many people. They were firing with spray guns and 'So was I,' but their sprays were not affecting me because I was carrying;

The Light of God

The rays of light were coming out of my hand. I stopped their firing with light and fired at them with the spray guns and made them disappear into thin air. After fighting for a long time, their firing did affect me. The effect of firing on my body was; first, my hair turned into a silver colour. Then your hair becomes so hard like the spines on a hedgehog. After that, the body goes frail and disappears into thin air.

After a long fight, I asked my fellow man, Mr Dhaliwal, 'How do I look? he said, yes, you are affected; your hairs are turning silver and his were too. I said, wash your face with cold water and he did but I had a positive attitude. After that, we were trapped in a big castle, with high walls and big gates but all were closed. It seemed like the end of this physical world. I knew in the back of my consciousness that this fight was not in the present time. The word **'Future'** flickered many times.

There were thousands of people inside and we were trying to break the gates using big guns. I said to my partner, don't worry, the gates will break; get ready to escape. The forces were all around. I looked at my partner and said, I will help you here and in heaven. I am the Present Living Master. After I said that, everyone began to feel good and get back to their normal health, me too. The gates broke off and everybody was free and healthy.

Comment: This indicates something that will take place in the future. But nothing very shortly, I know the time.

TRIAD
Morning 24-2-1985

Spiritual Master myself and Paul Ji were in this experience and he was receiving some instructions from Paul Ji and acting on them. So, it was shown that it was all done with Paul Ji's agreement with whatever he was doing. There was no doubt that he is the present Living Master.

GOD'S CONSENT
Night 16-4-1985

There was a message for me from God; it was written.

'God Is Very Pleased With You'

Also, in the same experience, I was taken back to the times of 'Jesus Christ,' I did not meet Christ but met his disciples. I have met Jesus Christ a few other times.

PROPHET
Morning 18-4-1985

I received another message during my meditation. These exact words appeared on my third eye screen.

'You are going to be a prophet.'

It was a short and awe-inspiring message.

❦

PAUL JI VISITS 'LIVE'
2-8-1985

I was in my factory near the new warehouse, where Mr Sidhu used to strap the pallets. I saw Paul Ji coming towards me and I began to walk towards him. We hugged each other; To me, everything looked very cheerful. I knew that October 1986 was approaching. We had a long conversation.

❦

FED UP IN THIS WORLD
Sat. Morning 3-8-1985

I am fed up today about everything in this world, society and the work we have to do for our survival. I thought we were not here to work, make a living and forget our real goal.

Which most people are not even aware of. I don't like families or businesses; there is no freedom. I was so fed up that I could not sleep. I cried out to God, 'Why have you forsaken me and left me in this miserable world? I knew whatever I had been told was not true. I was thinking about some of the promises made to me in the past.

All I know; That I did not come into this world to work off my karma. I have been brought back for a purpose. So these people and this world do not attract me. It is tough to pass the time without any purpose. When all the promises are made and 1986 is coming near, you may be wondering. 'Why am I still fed up? As far as I am concerned, every moment that passes without a purpose is a waste of time.

When I went to sleep, the spiritual Master appeared in a dream state and he was giving something to the people; Some light. Light rays were coming out of his hand and after him, I came onto the scene, I took his place and I was doing the same. I can draw some conclusions about that. But within myself, something is telling me that something is not right that made me feel uncomfortable. 'We wait and see?

DIFFICULTIES OF MASTER

I remember all this and it is a good reminder from Paul ji book of the same title. It is not easy for that person under training and, above all, physical, mental and spiritual challenges. You cannot share your state of consciousness. You are alone, you may not be lonely but you know yourself that you are different. That is why Paul Ji called himself a cliff-hanger.

'It is True'

NEW LIVING MASTER
Morning 28-8-1985

During meditation, the experience opened up. I am going to be the new Master. I received the spiritual mantle and all the arrangements were made to introduce me to the public. The strange thing was that the spiritual power would not be exchanged on 22nd October. It will take place sometime in March or April.

I knew about it anyway, the meeting was arranged in a hall. I was also sitting in the hall with other people. I remember on the program it said; 'New Living Master.'

There was a spiritual Master and 100 Seekers in the hall. Once the spiritual power is given but before the introduction, he wasn't there.

I knew that he was not here anymore because I had already taken over that time. So in place of Dapren I got up and went onto the stage. Everybody clapped their hands. When I was about to make a speech, I woke up from my meditation.

LETTER TO DAPREN
Sunday 15-9-1985

The Ec...... organisation knew that October 1986 is approaching and that the master-ship would be changing. So, they executed all their plans to disable him from making any statement. They had already eliminated him from the organisation and told him not to use any copyright words.

I know from now on that this path is not going to be the same as it was initially at the time of Paul Ji. This path is not going to be beyond religion. All I know is that everything will be out of step.

(Copy)

Respected Master,

I have received your letter regarding what happened between the organisation and Sounds of Soul. It is quite all right, whatever your decision is, I'll agree with you. These words are only public domain. If I remember correctly, Paul Ji started this path with the name Bi-Location. We can find some positive words and we already have some. It is our inner feelings; when put together with words, they get spiritually charged.

There is no doubt that we are experiencing a significant setback. Only a few are responsible for this and many innocent Seekers are affected and misled. These few responsible people will have to pay for the total karma. I have had some good experiences recently. They show the future for us is bright and the time is approaching shortly. May the blessings be.

Yours in Spirit,

Comment: We are claiming that our teachings are beyond religion and we are the only closest path to God it could be. That means we have qualities similar to our creator. Any person who walks through our door for help, whether he is our member or not, 'Should not return empty-handed.' These two gentlemen are fighting over a few words which are not even theirs in the first place. These words belong to Sikhism. Paul Ji adopted these words for whatever reason, I don't know. I would not have done that.

IK-onkar is the first word of Guru Granth of Sikhism and this was the first word uttered into my ears when I was born. Paul Ji changed the spellings slightly and managed to copyright. It is not even ours or something out of our creativity in the first place; despite this, it is the only word in line with our teachings. The rest of them are a materialistic type or are not representing our teachings. I will not use them myself. Small references;

Rod: is a bar **of** steel and **Power** means to rule over someone.

Swords: men or warriors is again not in line with our teachings.

Mahant: As I said earlier, my background is from Nanak Sar Temple. There are hundreds of Nanak Sar Temples in this world. 'Do you know they have established one Mahant in each temple or at least one in each Country? You can enquire about this if you want to. 'Now I'll tell you, what Mahant

120

is? This person is well-grounded in their teachings and can translate the instructions into simple words for the listeners. He does not hold any spiritual power as such. So, adding an A at the end does not make it unique. **Mahanta; You may define his position as senior or high priest.**

I do not wish to be called '**Mahanta**' because it does not represent my state of consciousness. **I am so close to God that it has invested its pure love in me** so that I can reach every person in this world. I do not hold the Rod of Power, nor any person or saint is subordinate to me. God has invested free will within each Soul. No one is higher or lower other than the word **Karma**. I am just another Soul among others.

As they say, if you repeat something several times, it becomes the law. Our vocabulary should be godly and straightforward, down to earth, as we are saying that our teachings are closest to God. At present other religions are better in practice than us.

Sikhism: There are at least ten different branches and they all have their organisations. They share the same holy book, 'Guru Granth Sahib' and their ten gurus. I never heard them say; You can't use this or that.

Hinduism: There are uncountable branches; they all share Bhagavad-Gita, Brahma, Vishnu, Shiva and the rest of everything.

Christians: Are sharing Bible and Jesus Christ.

Islam: They have many organisations such as Sunni, Shia, Ahmadiyya, etc. They all share Qur'an and Mohamad.

Buddhism: Is spread in many countries, each practice in its way.

It seems like: America is fighting with everyone politically and spiritually. You have to ask their permission if you can breathe or not. **'You are beyond what?**

I request we act according to what we represent in this world; **God.** I explained all this to him at that time.

THE GURUS & GRANTH
Sunday 3.30 am 6-10-1985

Experience: I was shown the holy book of Sikhism – Guru Granth sahib. Guru Teg Bahadur was writing some shabads 'Words,' and they were discussing them. (I was reading the words too). Sri Teg Bahadur was telling his son, Sri Guru Gobind Singh, that later on, he should be writing his own words, which will help complete the Granth. It was a clear indication that Guru Gobind Singh was the last Guru and Granth would not be complete until his Bani was added to it.

'Then it will be complete.'

I was reading and listening as well. I had the privilege to meet them many times before and during the times when they were alive.

Blessed,

PARA-VIDYA 'LIVE'
Thursday11.52 am 10-10-1985

I was at work 'Factory' and alone then three Masters appeared before me, so now we were four.

Dapren, Fubi Kants, Myself & Newman

It was all about the 'God-Man,' and
a conversation arose as follows;
'Newman' said to Dapren: 'Is it coming to me?
Spiritual Master said: No.

Fubi Kants points at me, 'Sher Gill' and says:
It is going to him.

It was a very short and to-the-point experience.
Then they all left.

MEDITATION & SATSANG
Wednesday 4.30 am 6-8-1986

I woke up at 4.30 am from asleep and sat down for meditation; I woke up from my meditation at 5.30 am and began to read the Satsang discourse. Once that finished, I went back into meditation because I didn't know what else to do. This is my first love and life.

Some people have played all the tricks in the book. I have not bothered to write about my experiences between 10-10-1985 till 6-8-1986 because now the whole teaching system is upset.

Comment: What I feel at the moment is that; the spiritual guardians appointed by the Spirit have turned the pure teachings into a big '**Joke.**

Those who are responsible, 'Will they pay
for this unplanned change?

MISSION
Morning 10 am 26-8-1986

'Can you believe the situation that I am in? As you will notice throughout my diary, I have been the pivot of the whole organisation and holder of the highest state of consciousness. Yet I am not able to utter a single word to anyone to say who I am and what I know. The people around me don't know what I am going through or who I am. The people who know nothing are coming to tell me who the real Master is and often, 'I feel very similar to a puppet.'

I had a rather long conversation with Mr P. Singh about the organisation and the Master. He came especially to convince me that the 'Newman' is the real living Master. However, he had phoned me on 17-8-1984 to tell me that he had reported me to the new Master in writing. Today, he repeated the exact words that he had notified the new Master in writing that I am not their follower. This person is 'Soul Initiate.' I am not even complaining, even though they are coming to convince me.

We have been giving this message in meetings and seminars that this is an individual Path. We do not convince or convert anyone and do not enter anyone's psychic space without permission. When these people are running all over me, 'What teachings are they following? I want to know. Anyway, he tried very hard to convince me about the New Master. I told him, 'He is not my Master.' These are the people without any first-hand information; They do not even have second-hand knowledge.

He admitted that he has no experience regarding the present situation. I don't know why he is even bothering to convince me. These are the people who are led like sheep and help others do the same. After listening to him and knowing that he made a report on me, I still gave him my love and best wishes for his future followings. 'I like this old man, I don't know why?

NORMAL
'My opinion & decision'

I know the truth, who is the living Master and who will be the 'God-Man' but I said to myself, which I never did before, 'Why bother about this talk, who is the Master and who will be the Master? Forget about this hassle from now on and just be myself and spend the rest of my life as a normal person.

MISSION CONTINUES
Morning 1 am 27-8-1986

What I have written on the last page and what I have decided after what Mr P. Singh told me on 26-8-1986 leads to as follows;

Spirit & Paul Ji

Spirit watched me every moment of the day and night once Spirit became aware that I wanted to quit this mission. I was in meditation; the para-vidya opened up and Paul Ji appeared.

Paul Ji tried to convince me that I must carry on. I said; we have lost all the material to the big organisation and 'Dapren doesn't have much to give me?

'Where do I stand?

Paul Ji promised; that all the required materials such as books, letters and discourses would be given to you. You will have your own material.

I said: OK.

I know what Spirit was hinting at; I am not here to spend an ordinary life; I am here to fulfil a mission.

Comment: You may notice from my times of meditation; for example, this one is at 1 am that I meditate at any time. I know, I am very crazy spiritually. I want to tell you that if you wish to have any success, half-hour meditation will not lead you anywhere. I'm afraid I have to disagree with other Masters 'What they said.'

'This is the only way'

———————————————

MISSION OR SUBMISSION
Saturday 3.57 am 28-10-1986

This is the mission but Spirit turned my mission into submission to make me say 'Yes' so that I could not walk away in the future. I was with two other Seekers and my father. The place was our village. We were walking in the direction shown in the sketch. Then suddenly a helicopter crashed as it was coming down at a very high speed.

It was like a 3 ft cube solid piece of metal crushed together as they did in scrap yards when it dropped. It dropped right at my feet but it touched my right arm first; I thought it must have damaged it but it was slightly bruised but not hurt when I looked at my forearm properly. It was clearly shown what happened to the big organisation and my mission.

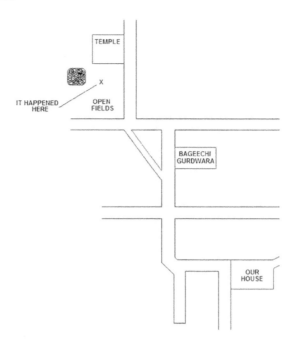

As I was giving up, Spirit came after me to ensure that I did not. After a while, something else begins to zoom on top of us, especially on me. It was a bowl about 7 ft diameter and made of pure illuminated white-silver colour. It made circles around us and tried to drop on me, I jumped back and it returned. This time it was very low, about 3 ft above ground; I plopped down on the floor and escaped.

Last time, this bowl came in at a very high speed but this time it came in at a very slow speed and about one ft above the ground. I lay down on the ground; it came slowly near me. I was repeating the spiritual word and it landed right on top of me. The Spirit bowl was right on top of me, covering me in total; inside, I was alone. I could feel that I was in the hands of Spirit and surrounding me. Inside or under the Spirit bowl, I felt great but very mature spiritually.

THIS WAS THE SHAPE   I LAYED ON THE GROUND

After a while, the Spirit bowl lifted and tilted to one side. I was in a sitting position, 'sitting on my knees' I was asked or told by the Spirit to write down what I am and let people know, 'Who I am? Before speaking to them. I had reddish-brown chalk in my hand and I wrote on the ground.

'I am the Living Master and God-Man'

THE LIVING MASTER AND PRABH-GUR

As soon as I had done that, the Spirit bowl was gone. At this time, the people were very eager to see me and look at me. I was quiet; my feet were on the ground, yet I felt that they were above ground. People gathered from all over; one man said please help me and another repeated this. People were waiting for me to give the message. I was just about to speak when Spirit woke me up and said, 'It is meditation time.'

'I said thank you'

GOD, MYSELF & A CHILD
Morning 15-11-1986

Experience: Spirit has shown me the present situation on this path. I was lying in bed and on one side, there was a big fellow like a man lying beside me. I could feel his presence was like a God. Then I felt someone else come and lay on the other side of me but I felt his hand like a child. I was lying in the middle of two, God on one side and a child on the other side.

After a while, the big fellow 'God' got up and checked what was lying beside me. It looked at the child and said; this child does not look like yours. I don't think he belongs to you. When I looked properly, it was 'Kal' as a child. I tried to push him away from my bed but he begged for mercy. The big fellow also agreed with me to push him away.

After that, we talked about Dapren. The big fellow 'God' told me that he is trying to sort out the present situation but that it is a big mess. Also, God said to me that it might be about time to bring you 'Master' into the open at one point. I said; Thank You.

THE MESSAGE OF 3 GIANTS
7.30 am 9-12-1990

As nothing was materialising spiritually, I did not bother to write about any experiences, although I received many. So, I thought, 'Why bother? This morning three giants came, so I was in an excellent mood to record what they said. There were only a few listeners but they listened very carefully to what I was saying.

I was telling them that Guru Nanak, Baba Nand Singh and my spiritual Master ordered me to keep all children happy, which means the whole creation of God.

All listeners were pleased that these three spiritual giants had given me this duty. So, I must look after all the Souls and keep them happy in every possible way.

NEGATIVE SPIRIT
3.30 am 20-2-1991

There was a place with many temples. They were all made of marble, built by individual families or some by big organisations. Most of them were built very nicely in these shapes. People came to pay their respects and take their bows but these temples were not clean. It seemed that nobody looked after them but one temple was the biggest.

People of that temple 'Negative Spirit' want me to look after it. Then I was told that they had taken my name off their list. They were told they could not have me because I was needed somewhere else.

UNCOMPLETED MISSION
5-6 pm 18-1-1991

A large number of people gathered in my village. There was a saint, he greeted me and I kissed his hand in respect, there were two other people present but I do not recall who they were.

The saint was Sikh in appearance and he said that there would be a replacement for baba Nand Singh of Nanak Sar. People did not understand what he said but I knew he was pointing at me internally. At the same time, I had the feeling that I was going to replace Paul Ji as the God-Man. There was some kind of information that Baba Nand Singh and Paul Ji had left their mission. One of them said it had to be completed by myself, 'In five to six years.' So, we were talking about 1996 To 1997.

There were two Punjabi Kurtas (shirts) of light green colour and hanging on a clothesline. My father asked, 'What is this? Probably he did not like them. Then somebody told him that Baba Nand Singh and Paul Ji had given them to me. Then he said; Why no one had told him before. Then he loved them.

Now two shirts of two great saints, I wonder what these two saints have in common.

As I am the only person to replace both

PURITY
6 am 18-3-1991

It was a short and clear-cut experience. I was told that I am as purified as Nectar 'Amrit' it was said in Punjabi;

'Amrit Ki Tranh Pavitar Hai Tu'

NEW CORPORATION
10-8-1991

My father was building a big house; I noticed that a few bricks were missing. I knew that Master was preparing for a new corporation, almost ready.

BY – LAW
Sunday Morning 11-8-1991

During this experience, I was shown that I had left my family. I am a saint and living in the USA. Our Master was making the transfer of 'spiritual power' through the courts and declaring everything through the newspapers. Then I found myself back in England with my family and I was showing them all the newspaper cuttings and they were all happy.

SEEKER'S EXPERIENCE
Monday Morning 12-8-1991

This Seeker and I were discussing experiences and he said; I have few experiences. I said I have got two whole books of experiences. He said, 'Can I have a look? I said; No. He said;

We are all Seekers. I said; Yes but you can look at them when the right time comes. Then everyone can read them.

This Seeker has hinted that he has some experiences with me on many occasions. Every time I knew what he was going to say. I always gave him an evasive answer and tried to cut down the conversation. As I knew, it was not the right time to discuss it any further.

DAPREN IN LONDON
Sunday 7.40 am 22-12-1991

Experience; He came to England. I went to see him in the hall, we met and after a short while I came home. I gathered my family and went back to see him again so that they could also meet him. We were standing in the queue and slowly moving closer to the Master; I was thinking about how to introduce my family.

I said to myself, I will say, this is my family. Then I decided to say; this is our family. When I reached where he was meeting people, someone else was sitting there. Master had left a message that he had gone to London. To see someone to inform them that he is changing the spiritual mantle and handing it over to Sher Gill. He will be back very soon and asked me to wait for him.

PRESENT SITUATION
13-2-1992

It was regarding the present situation between Master and the New Man. In the experience, as being the living Master, he said to me that he had given them two years or else!

'It was a short experience'

Later Comment: Nothing happened.

DEPRESSION TIME
3 am 18-2-1992

Experience: I was walking on top of snakes; wherever I went, I could not help putting my foot on top of these snakes. They were all fighting to bite me; lots of them had a go at my legs and were doing their best. I was careful but a child's voice 'Spirit' said, They cannot harm you, don't worry. It was regarding my present life situation that I am going through as a person. I have lost interest in everything; There is nothing that attracts me.

Life as a whole had gone dull and it was a depressing time. I feel alone; family, friends, money and jobs all are of no use. The Spirit appeared again in the shape of a child and God-like. 'The time is near,' I asked, 'How long or near? The child

'Spirit' said, we are not supposed to tell you but I insisted; the answer came three years.

'I said ok'

Comment: As you can imagine, after going through my experiences, it is not easy to be a spiritual man and a physical man. The time before becoming the living Master is very tough. After becoming the Master is even more challenging. It's not a bed of roses, as some people believe. During my waiting, an excessively long period is like a rubber band. As they say, one more stretch and it is going to snap. All I can say now is, 'So what? Let it be.

GOD'S BLESSINGS
15-3-1993

After a long time, I am writing this experience; so many experiences have gone unrecorded. As I said before, 'Who cares? During the meditation, one old saint appeared. He began to give my future forecast. God is pleased with you; it has given you his special blessings. Just chant his name directly in your meditation, no one else's. I am not sure what else I was told.

GRAND FATHER
2-4-1993

I am the present living Master and we were holding some kind of meeting and my grandfather came to attend the meeting to give support. He passed away in 1989. He was a jolly older man, very moderate, well qualified in his time and a real gentleman. I do miss him sometimes.

TWO CHAKRAS
Morning 6-4-1993

In this experience, I was shown that I have two Crown Chakras in my head, as shown in the sketch. Two open spots on top of my head where spiritual experiences take place. Maybe this is 'Why' my Soul body does not stay in for too long in my physical body. This is very rare or extraordinary.

BRITISH PASSPORT
Morning 10-4-1993

During this experience, the spiritual Master informed me that I would be moving to the USA after transferring the spiritual mantle. He suggested that I get a British Passport, it would make it a lot easier to travel the world. At present, I have an Indian Passport. Although I am a permanent resident of the UK, I was reluctant to change my passport because I have a big farm in India.

Later: Now I have gained a British Passport.

THREE REMINDERS
Morning 4-2-1994

I had three different experiences in one night and all expressed the same, I am the living Master and I was also told the same. I have been reminded time after time of my mission and encouraged to uplift myself spiritually.

ALL SAINTS
Morning 4-3-1994

In this experience, I talked to my father and he said we are blessed by all saints who have been here throughout history, up to now.

Comment: I am one of the first five people on this earth planet. So I am as old as time and history. So, all the saints have come and gone during my time here on earth.

BABA ISHER SINGH
Morning 7-3-1994

This is one of the saints I visited at Nanak Sar during my childhood. He came to see me. He is very much my regular visitor and I hold a lot of respect for him. I had learned a lot from him earlier. Nowadays we exchange our views, he was here a few days ago but on that day we did not exchange any words. Sometimes silence is golden.

EUROPEAN SEMINAR
Morning 11-3-1994

This information was given to me in advance about what will happen at the European seminar in England. We were attending a spiritual seminar and spiritual Master was there and all other known Seekers in England. After the seminar, Miss S. A. came to see me, gave me a bag and said that Master has sent you this Parshad 'Blessed food.' I checked inside the bag; there were Indian sweets known as 'Ladoo' I took one out and ate it.

'Blessings from Spirit'

Later: Yes, very similar blessings did take place but in a different manner.

HOUSE IN HEAVEN
Monday Morning 4-7-1994

During the meditation, I heard a voice similar to the spiritual Master saying; all the hard work you have done, you will be rewarded tomorrow. I was carrying a basket full of small beautiful grapes without bunches. They looked exceptional, like diamonds or pearls.

At the same time, I had the feeling that the result is positive. I was doing a job at Mrs Thandi's house; mid-day, we had a cup of tea. We were having a conversation about this path and she remarked to me. She said I have seen your spiritual house being built in heaven. It was so big and beautiful. It is very hard to explain and it is still being built more.

'I Said Thanks'

On Wednesday, during another break, she revealed her friend experience named Rani (Swaran). She was also building a house in heaven but she was told that everybody should build a house like Sher Gill's house.

THE TIME
Early Morning 21-10-1994

If you check my diary thoroughly, I don't think you can count the number of times that promises have been made. 'It makes me wonder sometimes? **'If Spirit cannot maintain a promise, then who can?** It does bring doubts into your mind. Despite being a severe believer in Spirit, it does create frustration. I feel deficient due to some bad experiences and past experiences. I feel frustrated because of the special restrictions I live in this world.

I am thinking of breaking them; 'When is my turn coming up? I am fed up living with these conditions and waiting for my turn. I said to myself; so what, forget the whole thing and begin to lead an everyday life like everyone else. You may wonder what the restrictions are; They are all beyond human description. On the physical, you cannot let a single Iota of negativity in your state of consciousness.

You cannot go in the street and have your fun or do 'hoo-haa-haa' like anyone else or any physical activity that the Spirit does not support. If anything is out of order, the spiritual hand is always hanging around your ear to slap you. You cannot go and have an alcoholic drink, fight, bully someone, cheat someone or tell lies and the list is endless. Sometimes, I wonder why Spirit kept its hand around my ear to slap when it did not apply to people before me or those who are doing against me.

You must be a picture of purity and an example to others. Anyway, early in the morning, I heard Master's voice saying, 'You have to study for one more year.' This experience is similar to my previous experience, dated 18-12-1992; maybe it is not recorded in this diary. We will wait and see. I believe in things only when they happen.

SPIRIT
Early Morning 1-11-1994

During meditation, at 3 am, the experience opened up. I am walking alone and a child begins to follow me. The child must be about 8 to 9 years old. He kept following behind me with an insistent attitude. The face was filthy, as though it had not been looked after properly; it is only a symbol, so I was kind to him. I held the child and washed his face. The face was so beautiful. I just kept looking at it. This child was still with me and said, 'Will you feed me from now on?

'Spirit' was asking for my word on this.

I said: Yes, I will.

I woke up from the meditation. 'Blessed'

FUTURE DESTRUCTION
7 am 9-11-1994

In this experience, I received a forecast for big destruction that will happen in this world in 35 years. So it makes approximately the year 2029 / 30 or near about because the exact date is not given.

GOOD FEELING
10 pm 9-11-1994

I just had a good feeling about an Image.
There is an Image,
There is a reflection of the Image in water,
The reflection can be disturbed by someone throwing a stone,
'So why not become the Image, instead of the reflection?

GOAL
Early Morning 19-11-1994

During meditation, Master appeared at the third
eye and said;

'Now you have achieved your goal.'

Comment: I don't know how many times
I have to achieve my goal.

THE VOICE
12 noon 18-1-1995

I was in meditation at noon and a short
experience popped in. **'It asked**?

'Are you the Voice of God?

I said: Yes.

God asked me to give my word on this,
so I always act in its' obedience.

Blessed

FLYING POSTER
Sunday am 18-1-1995

It was early morning and I was just about to have my breakfast. It was already prepared by my Mrs and left on the table in my absence as I was in the bathroom. Normally she brings it when I am ready and out of the bathroom. So I missed meeting her face to face. So, I thought, 'Which family member will I see first today? I never thought of these terms before. Maybe Spirit wanted to give me this experience.

I was just thinking about it and then suddenly a poster, which Dapren had sent me; it had been lying on the cupboard shelf since Christmas. It began to float in the air; I put my hands together and the poster landed in my hands facing upwards.

'Master's picture facing and looking at me'

I was pleased, that I saw the Master first this morning. It is amazing, what Spirit can do and how quickly it can answer back.

NB: The distance from the position of the stationary poster on the cupboard shelf to my lap was approximately 8ft. There was no window open or Fan working in the room. 'What made the poster fly? As I said earlier, it is amazing that everything is possible in this little room.

THE WALK
6.40 pm 1-7-1995

Look ye not in front,
Look ye not behind,
Look ye not to left,
Look ye not to right,
Look ye among yourself,
Look ye within yourself,
It is your Master.

I AM GETTING OLD
1-7-1995

I was thinking about my age, due to the change of spiritual power because I have been reminded too many times.

'You are next in line'

I do think it is better; if it is given to someone younger so that he can carry on for a longer period. Anyway, that's that and I feel very sad sometimes as well. What is happening in this world and I am helpless to do anything. Later a short experience came as follows;

It is your turn next,
With age comes maturity.

Comment: I am just wondering, 'How much more do I have to mature?

SADNESS
Morning 2-7-1995

In this experience, I was given the spiritual power by Spirit and guess; 'Who was looking over? It was someone who didn't want to know.

'He wasn't a happy man'

CHANGE OF DATES
5-8-1995

1. Two short experiences took place. I am told that the change of spiritual mantle will not take place in October as usual; I am not sure if the message was December or January.

2. Another message was that I am next in line, so it is my turn.

MANIFESTATION
Early Morning 9-11-1995

We were having a meeting in the seminar hall. The spiritual Master was supposed to come but he was late. It was about time to begin the seminar and we were all getting anxious for him. The audience was also waiting for us to begin. I was at the back of the stage area and then the Master's face started to appear in front of me and then the whole body. Master's entire body manifested there and then.

He moved from there to the front of the stage and he sent the message for me through a Seeker Miss S. A. to tell me that I should go home and change into new clothes. I went home to change clothes. It was a hint for me to stay ready; it was about time to transfer the 'spiritual mantle' to me.

SPIRIT AT WORK
18-1-1996

I was standing in open fields and I was going to cultivate that area. Then I saw two baby snakes sitting on a tree branch and looking at me. I did not want to kill them, so I told them to leave. They left and shortly afterwards, hundreds and thousands more came out of the soil where I was standing and they all left the area. To let me get on with my work, I was amazed.

'I think it is a good sign'

THE BOOK
Saturday 7.15 am 18-5-1996

Experience: There was a spiritual meeting and a bookstall. There were several Seekers; after some time, they all went home. One lady Mrs Narinder told me that she wanted to buy a small book and after that she went home too. However, I was supposed to bring a small book for her later. When I was about to do that Paul Ji appeared and he handed me the same book but in a large size. I said to myself, 'I will keep this big book and give my copy, which was smaller in size, as she wanted the small book.

Paul Ji gave me the book, I asked him if he could kindly autograph it. He agreed and I opened the page with Paul's picture on it. Paul Ji autographed it under his photo. The autographed was in this manner 'Sketch' in the shape of a tree and signed 'Brish,' which means tree in India and he handed the book over to me. Then I closed the bookstall in an ample space like a dockyard at **'Rahakajah'** Camalot. Then Paul Ji and I turned the lights off for the whole area because it was closing time. So we both left.

Later addition as a comment, I am often amazed how Spirit works. This lady 'Narinder' approached me on 26 April 2011 to say, 'The new Master is supposed to give me a book.' I told her I had already given you the book back in 1996. So now I have given her 'The Way to God' signed exactly as Paul Ji signed it for me.

GOODBYE
15-3-2001

I was on holiday in India and Paul Ji came to see me. He slapped his hand on my hand like saying goodbye and it seemed like he was going somewhere.

YOU CAN'T HIDE
Morning 23-3- 2001

For a long time, I had stopped writing about my experiences. 'I don't know why? Probably, I got fed up with the whole idea. Yes, there were some reasons for it. Anyway, this morning two different experiences took place because I had been told too many times by Paul, Rebazar and other spiritual Masters and none of the dates come true. It seemed like more than a cat and a mouse game to me.

I requested Spirit that I would be grateful if Spirit could choose somebody else. Someone younger, so this person can serve Spirit for a longer time. So positively, I wanted to give up and began to plan my retirement.

Experience; This time, Paul Ji came and looked at my face for some time and he noticed that there was one black spot on my cheek, 'like a beauty spot' karma. He lifted his hand, removed that black spot and told me that he could not find anybody else. It made me wonder, what happened to those 85 people 'Who were said to be under his training? Dapren made this statement during one seminar in Europe. I was surprised to learn that there were so few people with this state of consciousness.

Comment: When he made this statement, I was sitting in the audience at that time. I said to myself, 'What is he talking about? When I knew it was not true.

One hour later, the Master came up in a very short experience. He looked at me and said,

'Now It's Time'

LIGHT
Thursday 6 pm 14-11-2002

Today I have read 2/3 discourses and done a bit of meditation and I feel lazy. I felt like having a short nap. As I lay down on the sofa, I had an experience with other members but nothing much to remember, at the end of the experience or before waking up.

A light appeared on the third eye, it was pure white light; I looked at it for a while and it slowly disappeared and then I woke up.

LIGHT
5-12-2002

During meditation, a light appeared in the spiritual eye; I watched it for some time and then it faded slowly.

START WORKING
7-12-2002

I said 'No' to accepting the future master-ship over the last few years. I am fed up with the whole idea and the life situations that I had been put through. It has been one thing after another. My son had an accident this year, an extraordinary experience after the accident and an even stranger one after he got well. I was very disappointed about the accident and the mental torture. Which has been created around me; then, one day in December, I gathered my energy and made up my mind. Now it does not matter what happens to me or my family or anything else.

I have been given this birth, especially for this purpose and I have to continue my goal. 'Now, it does not matter what?

I have to do it for the Spirit and myself. On the same day during my meditation spiritual Master came and said, 'Thank God you have woken up now,' and then he said,

'Start working'

LAST TWO INITIATIONS
9-12-2002

Two days later, the spiritual Master appeared again and said; although I gave you the 12ᵗʰ initiation back in 1981, due to your giving up the idea, you have lost two steps. So I will charge you again spiritually to the same level. He gave me the 11ᵗʰ and 12ᵗʰ initiation again and I said, 'Thank you for the gift.

NEXT PAUL JI
13-12-2002

I had doubts about my ability to be the next Master, especially since Paul Ji knew so much. He received special training from Rebazar Tarz and other spiritual Masters. 'Where do I stand if I become the next spiritual Master? During meditation, an experience opened up;

'Next one will be as good as Paul Ji was'

This was the answer to my conversation with Spirit during the daytime.

THE WILL OF GOD
2-1-2003

I sometimes wonder, 'Why me? I was thinking about myself, 'Who am I? I am not special or I don't see it that way. I am sure there must be many other people in the world who can take the master-ship. The experience came with some explanation and the last spoken words were;

It is 'The Will of God' to choose you as the next one.

'Blessed'

UPGRADING
3-1-2003

In this experience, the spiritual Master said, It is time for upgrading; I knew he was talking about master-ship.

MRS SATWANT KAUR
3-1-2003

Sadly, her son passed away on 2 January 2003 and she was worried sick. I went into meditation from 7.30 am to 11.30 am and woke up 2-3 times in the middle of it due to some disturbances.

On the soul plane, I met her husband, who passed away a few years ago. I saw his house and we discussed his son. Who had managed to land on the causal plane according to his karma. Bells were ringing in the background and I saw the beautiful pool and I told her what I had seen and she was pleased. I described the exact looks of her husband, whom I had never met or seen his photograph on the physical.

Mrs Satwant Kaur has now passed away. She always treated me like her own son and I always felt that she was my mum too. 'God bless her.'

BIG HOUSE
1-6-2003

My house was being built. I wasn't doing much work myself to build it. Other people, such as our Seekers, were doing the job and it was so big, bigger than my requirements.

TIME IS SHORT
3-6-2003

Experience: There were four of us doing the building work for me. I was bringing bricks in a wheelbarrow. The spiritual Master was on the building site, doing the work himself. I was getting the material so fast and he was even faster than me. Every time I brought the wheelbarrow the previous material had already been used up. I am trying to say that whatever I was building, it needed to be built fast. The spiritual Master was pleased with whatever he was doing. It seemed like time was running out and a new time was approaching.

TIME UP
5-11-2003

During meditation, the spiritual Master said, 'It's only two to two and half months left.' I mark it as the middle of January 2004. Now I requested Spirit to allow me some time because I had unfinished work at home. Once I start my future assignment, I do not want to look back. I hope that Spirit will allow me some more time but if Spirit wants me now, 'How could I refuse?

So many experiences have taken place and remained unrecorded. He is doing an excellent job; the longer he carries on, the better it is for me. I wish he would carry on forever so I didn't have to become the Master.

I NODDED YES
Thursday 3.10 am 23-1-2004

Today spiritual Master called me and I was with him and another 30 to 40 Seekers. He said to me;

'You know why you are here?
I nodded yes

Then he said because you are taking over as the next Master. Shortly afterwards, the experience stopped and I woke up. The spiritual Master returned 'same morning' at 5.15 am and said, 'I am ready to hand over the power if you agree to receive it.' I requested Spirit again to give me a few more months.

Later I was given another date.

HOVERING PAUL JI
1-4-2004

I could feel often during the day that Paul Ji is around and during the night time. I was wondering why Paul Ji was hovering around today. I did not see him but I knew it was him. A short experience came when Paul Ji wanted to make sure that I was fully trained for the job.

PAUL JI & PSYCHIC
5-4-2004

Paul Ji was again at his job of training me. I am not sure what had taken place as everything was in the background; All I could feel was that lots of psychic power were being pumped into me. Once he finished, I became conscious again.

———— ❦ ————

EXPERIENCES
5-1-2005

For some months, I had not seen much that I could remember. Every time I began to read or meditate, I went into deep samadhi straight away and remembered nothing much.

I had been saying this to myself, 'For God's sake, what is going on? Early January 2005 I was told about the mastership. That I was put on hold for a year, as I requested. Now I know the background; the word 'God-Man' appeared in my third eye and during the meditation. I was also told;

'You are slipping on the 13th Initiation'

I said to the spiritual Master, 'Why don't you help me sort this out? For a few days, I wondered, 'What is the problem? Then one day, I was nudged within by the Spirit that I am

159

not maintaining my higher state of consciousness all day. So, I am not even allowed to waiver for a little while. I must maintain my state of consciousness up to the fourteenth plane. After that, the word 'God-Man' appeared in my third eye; probably that is my reward.

ANOTHER EXPERIENCE
7-1-2005

Some of the Seekers, such as Rani and Mrs Thandi, were on a visit to a spiritual seminar in America. Then Master ordered Miss S. A. to take me with her from England. The Seekers discussed that they knew who was coming with Miss S. A.

'Of course, mentioning my name.'

RANI CAME TO OUR HOUSE
11-1-2005

Rani came to see me and told me a negative story about Dapren and something else. A rumour spread by a known Seeker that he is no more. I disagreed because we are always in touch with each other, as you can see throughout my diary. I told her, 'I will find out,' So I meditated and managed to contact him about what I saw! He had gone a bit into a child-like state and his head 'skin' was wounded from nail marks.

160

It means that either he had scratched himself or was a sign of internal wounds. Then I meditated and requested God, Satnam Ji, Paul Ji and other known Masters. To protect the Master because he would not ask for it. During meditation, Paul Ji came up wearing metal armour, similar to the armour that English knights used to wear. So it was a sign that Paul Ji had taken responsibility. I was also shown that about 40 to 50 Seekers are looking after him. I am not sure if they are in physical or in soul bodies.

MORNING
17-1-2005

I was shown that Master's head wounds had not healed but the body was ok. So that means he was getting better.

'Well, Good News'

SPIRITUAL RESPONSIBILITY
Morning 1-3-2005

This time I was in India on my holidays and during the meditation, the spiritual eye experience opened up. Spirit came and gave me spiritual responsibility as Master's health deteriorated. So I was told to take over the spiritual side of the responsibility. To sum up, God spoke in Punjabi, my mother language;

'Teri Bhagti Hun Puri Ho Chucki Hai'

It means that 'Now you have achieved your spiritual goal.'
Or
'You have reached your spiritual destiny.'

VOICE OF GOD
Thursday 6.54 am 9-8-2005

I was standing in front of a form or
formless sort of being; **God**
I could see,
Yet I cannot describe,
The voice of God came and said in Punjabi;

'Meri Pavitarta Da Khial Rakhna'

Means; Look after my purity.

I received consent from God and I said;
'Yes'

Then I became conscious again from my meditation

Thank you, God

MONTHLY REPORT
30-08-2005

Respected Master

I have almost completed 29 years under your supervision I want to thank you from the bottom of my heart and family. Your guidance has been priceless. The journeys we have done together and guidance on the physical have given joy and happiness to my family and friends. More than 50 percent of your advice has produced miracles on the physical and the rest on a spiritual level.

Lots of my friends, family members and Atom Seekers are witnesses to this. They have enjoyed and appreciated your help and guidance. We cannot thank you enough even if we try. Your presence in this world is the biggest miracle itself. I have always looked at you as my father. You have been a good friend and companion through your presence which I can feel. I have never felt alone in all these years.

We had a spiritual dinner yesterday, 29-08-2005, at our house; everybody was happy and thankful to you. Thank you from myself and our family.

Yours in Spirit,

SPIRITUAL MANTLE PICTURE
3-3-2006

An experience by Myself & my wife: P. K. Gill

There is Darwin's spiritual mantle picture on our bedroom wall. Somehow in a dream, P.K. was looking at this picture and all Masters began to come out of the picture frame one by one. Eventually, they all went out of the picture frame. Now the picture frame was empty. Then suddenly, she witnessed that all the Masters were in our house and most of them were downstairs in the sitting lounge.

Dapren, Paul, Rebazar, Rami Nuri, Gopal Das and Lai Tzes, there were more Masters than you could count. They were standing and walking about in the house as they pleased. There was not a single person from outside and there was not much exchange of words between the Masters.

Later she came upstairs and looked at the rod of the power picture frame once more. This time picture frame was not as empty as before but there was plain white paper within the frame. All clean but without a picture of any Master as they were all downstairs 'Live' with me having a meeting or discussing Spirit. As you know, I hardly slept; at the same time, she was dreaming exactly the way we were downstairs. It was a clear indication that 'This is their home' from now on. It is unbelievable how Spirit works.

DARSHAN MANIC
9-3-2007

He was my best friend who introduced me to this spiritual path. Later due to the organisation's split, he remained Eckist while I was with Atom. Our friendship remained the same; we never said to each other why you followed him or him. We consistently applied the term; Be yourself and let the others be. This is what I call an Eckist. If we cannot accept each other on this path, then there is no way you will accept other religions. He passed away from this world on 9th March 2007; I am sure he would have been very happy for me, where I am today.

RUDE AWAKENING
20-6-2007

I call this a rude awakening because it took me almost 40 years to realise what had happened. As I mentioned in my book, I used to go to Nanak Sar Temple after leaving school. I used to walk 3 miles and stay overnight and come back in the morning to attend school. On 20 June 2007, I was shocked to realise my past younger years to which I had never paid much attention before. My first love of life is and has been God and if there is any second, that is to look after my physical body; in other words, I love sports.

I played every possible game available to us in the village, such as; Running catch-catch, marbles, hockey, kabaddi and wrestling. I still remember playing these games in the evenings and all the places we were. I remember all the names of my friends who were playing with me regularly. I can go over and over the alleyways that we ran through every day.

After 40 years, I discovered, out of the blue, 'A vision struck to reveal,' that this happened during the exact same four years when I was supposed to be at the temple. 'Now, if I was at the temple then who was playing in the village at the same time? I still remember being at the temple at the same time as well. It shows very clearly that I had been at two places every day without even realising it. I haven't got a clue how it happened but it is true; that's how Spirit works. It shows very clearly that I happen to have two physical bodies.

It also shows that I am not as clever as many people think.

DARWIN LEAVING STAGE
USA Time; 10.35 am Saturday 8 March 2008

I felt as Spirit was guiding me to sit in meditation; as soon as I was done, that experience opened up. We were holding a seminar. I was on the stage and waiting for the Master to come on stage and make a speech. I saw him coming through the door on the right-hand side of the stage. As he came near me or the microphone to speak, I noticed that his face looked normal but there was lots of sweat on his face.

Darwin; 'Sher I am very tired.' (Exact words)

Sher Gill: 'Please go outside and have a break; when you are ready, then come back; in the meantime, I will manage.' (Exact words)

As soon as I said that, he turned around and began to make his way towards the same door. I kept watching him until he disappeared; as he walked towards that door, there was a bright white light around him.

When he came to me on the stage, I noticed his height was less than the original. In particular, his legs were very short and there were lots of sweat on his face. He said, 'I am very tired.' Is a sign through the symbols that physically, he was sinking. When he left this physical world and came to me to say goodbye. On Sunday 9th March 2008, a spiritual chant was held at Mrs Tembers' house. I indirectly conveyed to everyone present that Darwin was very sick. So, we did the spiritual chant for the Master's well-being.

Later: We did receive the letter from Bonnie Brant that Darwin had translated from the physical at 10.35 am Saturday, 8 March 2008. That was the exact time when I was in meditation in England. When he came to me to say a final goodbye, in Spirit, we are always together.

DARWIN & THREE MASTERS
15 March 2008

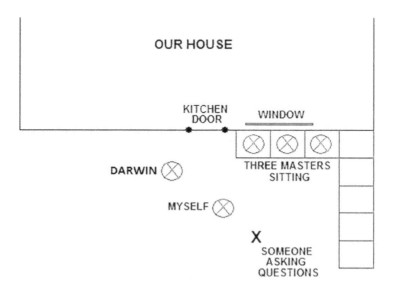

In our back garden, there is a sitting place which I made myself with bricks and slabs. Three spiritual Masters were sitting there and I was standing in front of them. Another person was standing on my right-hand side and he asked me, 'Who are they?

Sher Gill: They are our spiritual Masters.

As soon as I said that, they got up and one by one, they entered my body and stayed within me forever. Today, these three Masters, Darwin and myself, agreed on the 'Spiritual Word' for me to accept 'Spiritual Mantle' and Darwin to pass over the Spirit to me on 20 March 2008.

SHER GILL & SPIRITUAL MANTLE
20 March 2008

Darwin came along with those three Masters to my residence at the same place where I was standing in front of the three Masters on 15 March 2008. **'Spiritual Master Dapren'** moved forward, entered into my body and stayed there, never to come out on 20 March 2008.

'That was the transfer of Spiritual Mantle.'

OCTOBER 2008
6.30 am 22 April 2008

During meditation, a very short experience,
spiritual Master appeared and said;

'I'll see you on October 17th.'

'And he disappeared straight away.
There was nothing more or less said'

THANK YOU, SEEKERS

Later: Spiritual Master told me that all the arrangements had been made, which means some responsible people had been made aware of my coming. So, they can receive me and announce 'Who I am.' Unfortunately, no one approached me in this manner and according to my habit, I did not say anything to anyone. Once again, I was not in a position to declare myself 'trusting the spiritual information,' but nothing materialised in public. Although I am the present spiritual Master, I went into silence.

I would like to thank the five Seekers; My wife, Rani, Kuldip bhachu, Siso paul and Narinder Paul, who went with me to support. As they had their faith and trust in me because Spirit had shown them very clearly who I am. When I came back to England only a quarter of the Seekers believed; who I was. Some claimed that I was one of them sitting in their Satsang. If they somehow read my diary, they should feel lucky that I was sitting in their Satsang. I had such spiritual stamina I would not let anyone know, 'Who I am?

After Darwin's passing away; some Seekers came to know, 'Who I am? Out of jealousy, a group of known Seekers in England said, 'We are not going to let him become the Master.' It makes me wonder, 'What teachings have they been following over the last 30 Years? The conclusion is 'Nothing.' They are treating the teachings as if they are going to have some political debate and they are going to vote for or against me.

Some Seekers have left the teachings because they have lost their faith due to whatever has happened to this path. After reading too much negative material on the Internet, some Seekers have left the teachings. Those who provide the negative material on the Internet should not be ignored. They are only criticising the mistakes that we have made in the past. We should 'Thank them' and make sure that we do not repeat the same mistakes in the future. I believe that honesty is the best policy.

I love those people who believe in me as the living Master of the time. I also love those who don't believe in me. God has given free will to all of its creation, so I always believe in one thing, 'Be yourself and let the others be too.'

It is 'The Will of God'

'GOD'
Tuesday 5 pm 8-6-2010

I wanted to contact God today. I only managed to leave a message on the Inner. I did not want to come out of the meditation. As I was so leaned inwardly, then God took me directly into its' presence.

'I Felt Blessed'

'I did not want to but I came out of meditation at 6.15 pm.'

GOD'S WORLD
15-8-2010

What I have seen or been shown by God is unthinkable. Throughout spiritual history, it has been said; that it is not possible but with God's grace, it has taken place. I do not feel more special or better than anyone, nor did I make any special effort for this experience. It all happened with God's grace. It shows how much love God is holding for me.

'I Am Truly Blessed'

I feel very humbled to mention this and put it into the fewest words that I possibly can. The number of words I can use to explain will never be enough.

'Experience as follows'

This is the furthest a person can ever think or dream of but it will never materialise. You may be wondering what it could be. God took me into its' presence. It wanted me to follow; as I followed everywhere, up and down and side to side then **God said to me; This is the end of the other side.** For example, if the lowest is Physical, then 'This' will be the highest. The whole of the whole is like a balloon. We are all within an enormous balloon. I followed along with God; It was a never-ending circle.

Sher Gill: I could feel the inside of this balloon. I was touching it with my both hands. I tried to peep out of the balloon and poke my fingers into this rubber or jelly-type surface but I could not. The interior colour of this rubber or jelly was beautiful sky blue. So that was the end of the ends in that direction. I felt very much balanced; there was no such thing as excitement.

All I can say is that; I must be one of the most fortunate man in this world. As God has been so kind to me by showing all this, it is impossible according to this world's spiritual scriptures. **'As it did happen** then; **'What can I say?**

'All I Can Say Is, 'Thank You, GOD'

THE WAY TO GOD
31-12-2010

I have been doing my responsibilities on the physical and the spiritual side. It is the last day of the year 2010. I have been so busy all through this year and luckily, at last, I managed to have half a day spare for myself. I have been doing my physical chores to run the household and trying to write and get my first book, 'The Way to God' published.

So, on the last day of this year, I sit on the chair to open up the Internet for any general information on the religious side. Somehow Spirit directed me to look at the Ec..... organisations web site. Within minutes I was shocked to see the number of copyright words they have. Although, I have been very careful not to enter their psychic space.

On the other side, the publisher had sent me the email on 15 December 2010, saying that my book would be live within the next 7 to 10 days for anyone to purchase. I wasted no time sending them the email and explaining the legal side of the 'Words' and putting a stop to any printing and further sale. The two ladies I used to communicate with within the publishing department failed to respond. So, it came down to 4 / 5 January 2011; I managed to communicate with Author-house support.

At last, someone responded positively and understood my story. After 2 to 3 emails, I managed to put the book on hold. I told them that I would send them a new manuscript within a week and we could go forward from there. The Ec... organisation website mentions several copyright words and at the end, it says 'among others.' So, I felt more concerned about un-intentionally using copyright material and wanted to make sure what the other words were. 'Among others.'

So, I tried to find out the answer through a known Eckist. He said he was not aware himself, 'What are among others' words? He gave me the telephone number of the Ec.... organisations office and I contacted the legal department. Over the phone, I told her 'A-Lady' my story and requested if I could know what the other words were. She was not happy. The answer was, 'You have to come through your Attorney 'Solicitor' to know this.' I said, 'ok, thank you,' which was the end of that conversation. They operate more like a business when they should be kind and religious.

If she had told me, 'These are our copyright words,' then what had she to lose? It is beyond my knowledge. I would have said 'Thank You' very sincerely.

SPIRIT
Sunday 7.45 am 9-1-2011

I was lying down and had probably dozed off. I was beginning to get up to start my day when I realised that a tiny child was lying next to me on my right-hand side. I was in a semi-awake state. When I woke up fully, I realised that I was lying alone.

A small child is a symbol of a Spirit. As I was feeling a bit concerned about my book due to some legal points, it was shown to me that Spirit is with me;

'Have faith; Spirit is always with us.'

STATE OF CONSCIOUSNESS
Tuesday 4 am 29-5-2012

I had similar experiences that I am building a big house nowadays, sometimes huge and on a very large scale. It is a symbol of my state of consciousness. I don't pay much attention to this. All I know is, 'Just carry on doing what you can and leave the rest to Spirit.' Today I was with my father. The father figure is also a symbol of the Master or God.

I showed him around, I said; 'I will show you another house ready to be inspected.' As we entered the building, it was a

175

very bright white colour and he was concerned about its height. He asked, 'What is the height up to the ceiling? I replied, 'It is at least 14 ft; it may be more.' He was pleased to hear this. It was a sign of clearing my 14th Initiation on which I have been working for some time.

I AM ALWAYS WITH YOU

I have printed some of the experiences sent to me by our Seekers. I have lots in my file to show that Spirit is live and who the present Master is, as many claims to be. Any person can claim whatever they feel but how many karmas' you are committing, I don't think you have the slightest idea of it. I am living as always have been. I breathe through each of you and I breathe through the air and each particle of soil.

All the fruits of this world are evidence of my existence. All the lower worlds are part of an illusion. To market any illusion in this world is very easy; finance is the key. Illusion speaks louder than my silence, although, without my silence, nothing can exist. I breathe through the live spiritual channels, which are not many; if there are some, they are silenced by the pseudo-Masters. Their false actions give me a bad name and break the trust of those who want to believe in me.

I am always here to be experienced by anyone who makes up their mind. I am always so close to you, beyond your imagination. You do not have to be in any temple or church; I will show my presence in your home. This way, the torch of my silence will carry on forever. 'I am everywhere.' Whenever you can manage to raise your spiritual vibrations to cross the boundaries of illusion, my presence will shine through. What you see or hear in your visions are miracles to normal human minds.

All these experiences are printed with the
consent of the recipients.

Who is the new Master? 'Live'; I was going to attend the seminar in Cleveland, Ohio, 23 October 2008. Two weeks earlier, I was discussing the seminar with other Seekers. As the Master has already translated on 8th March 2008, we wondered 'Who the new Master is going to be? One of the Seekers asked me to request the Master. That evening, I stood in front of the Master's photograph and requested. If he could 'show me' who the new Master would be and where he would be located in the world.

Instantly, a brilliant white light appeared around the photograph and Sher-Ji appeared in a white suit in place of Darwin. I was pleased to know who the new Master is going to be. This was a live experience, which meant it did not occur while I was sleeping or meditating.   Mrs Seso Paul. Southall

Disappointed: On 23 October 2008, I went to Cleveland, Ohio, to attend the seminar. I expected Sher-Ji to be announced as the new Master because I was given the experience earlier. After the first day at the seminar, I had an experience during the nighttime. I saw a long staircase full of beautiful flowers in full bloom, as though the flowers were lining the route that the new Master would walk down. I felt wonderful. However, it quickly got dark and the experience ended.

I kept waiting for the new Master to be announced; however, no announcement was made. After the seminar, one day during meditation, one lady 'she was the responsible person at the seminar' appeared on the inner and said, 'I am very sorry' her face and her bearing made me feel that she was very sorry and regretting not doing what Master asked her to do. Swarn Kaur, Heston.

Master in Past Life: 'Live'; I was attending one of our spiritual-chant on Sunday. We do this chanting for the good of the whole, which is approximately for half-hour. We were very fortunate on that day as Sher-Ji was also present 'Physically.' We all decided to have a cup of tea and some sweets. I was holding the tray with sweets and offered everyone to have some.

As I approached Sher-Ji and offered these sweets, he only picked up a little bit. I requested, please have some more. He smiled and at the same time live experience opened up while I was standing in front of him. During that time, he showed me a number of his past lives. In one of them, he was a very well-known Master during the sixteenth century. While other Seekers were enjoying their cup of tea, I was totally out of this world and enjoying this experience a few centuries back.

Only a true Master can show and create this kind of experience or what we call a miracle. It was a very long experience but it may have happened in a split second compared with physical timing. Don't forget I was only making a round to offer some sweets. I will not be surprised if other Seekers may not even have noticed that I stood still in front of Sher-Ji. Master can show the whole Eternity in a split second. I was very fortunate to be in his presence that day. Mrs. Kuldip Bhachu, Southall

Live Presence: I was attending the spiritual chant at Mrs Seso Paul house. I saw Sher-Ji in brilliant white light during the spiritual chant in full body appearance. Physically he was not present that day. The Spirit blesses me. Mr Surinder Birk.

Divine Light: I was on holiday in India; I was doing my meditation and the experience opened up; I saw Sher Ji, guiding to show me the divine light. The light was so intense; I had never seen anything before. In the same experience, I saw many other lights as well, from gold to bright white and during this, I've seen Sher Ji in my visions simultaneously. In Spirit. Mr Surinder Birk, Ashford

Healings: Dear Sher-Ji, I have a wonderful experience a few days back. My husband had pains in his chest and we had to admit him to the hospital for one night. One of our dedicated Seekers stayed with me for help and moral support. In the morning, when we were doing our meditation, I had an experience that Sher-Ji was standing beside my husband's bed. You were wearing a blue shirt and your hand was on his shoulder.

I was pleased that Spirit was looking after him. After that, he got the all-clear from the Doctors to go home. I have no words to thank the Spirit; I am very fortunate to choose this path. I thank the present living Master for guiding me spiritually. We are fortunate to have your love and blessings. Mrs Rita Gill. London.

Satsang: I had been attending the Satsang for some time and managed to grasp precious knowledge by reading your book. Our Satsang teacher explains very well; overall, I am always looking forward to the next Satsang. What I learned later, once you participate from within or pass the boundaries of physical, then you enter into another dimension.

This is what happened to me very recently. We were sitting in the Satsang, I enjoyed it and our teacher made a very valid point. I could not help raising my head from the book to look at the teacher or how the point was being made. To my surprise, there was no teacher; instead, 'Sher Ji' was sitting and taking the Satsang. I was very fortunate to have the Darshan of your Radiant form; I was overwhelmed with happiness.

As soon as I turned my face to the side for a split second and turned around to see where you were sitting. Then to my surprise, everything was normal and our teacher was putting all the effort into explaining the subject involved. These experiences are only available on this path and only for the chosen ones by Spirit; the rest of the world will never understand. Fortunate one, Seeker. London

I saw you coming: 'Live': Sher-Ji, there was a spiritual chant at Mrs Narinder Tember's house recently. The majority of us were sitting inside. As I was sitting inside, suddenly I looked through the window, I saw you coming towards the front door but I did not see you physically inside the house. Now I know, at all spiritual chants, the Master is always there and when we invite other Masters, they are there too. What we get from the Spirit, I am always thankful. With spiritual love. Paramjit. S. Gill

Healings: 'Live'; My dear Master Sher-Ji; I will share some of the beautiful experiences you gave me. I am so blessed to walk, talk, breathe and sing with you. I cannot thank you enough for all your doings, without even realising you have supported me through thick and thin.

In the year 2008, I was told that I had a B. cancer; with your love, I got through it. One day some of our Seekers and yourself 'Sher Gill' came to my house to visit me. You sat a few steps away from me. I felt a warm glow of Vibrations coming my way from you. It was very uplifting; I felt at peace within myself. I knew the great Master had healed me; after that, my results from the hospital came all clear.

Thank you, Master-Ji, for listening, understanding and being such a special Master and a friend in my life. You took my pain and sorrows away to give me a new lease on life. Once again, I thank you from the bottom of my heart. I owe you one.

One of your dedicated spiritual Seekers. Mrs Gurnam. K. Birdi

YOU WILL NEVER SEE GOD

This applies to many or most of the people in this world. God is responsible for the whole creation; God has created us with love because it is within us and we are part of it. God loves you so much and it is responsible for every atom in our body and its well-being. We are breathing because God is living through us. God resides within each Soul; It does not matter if you are rich or poor, black or white. Or what religion you are following or even if you do not believe in its existence.

You are all welcome to be in its' presence, as long as you hold a universal approach or thought. As soon as you mention the word religion that you are Hindu, Sikh, Christian, Islam, Buddhist or any other, you have created the wall between God and yourself. You tell God that I know your existence but I am part of this religious system. Until you manage to rise above this thought, it does not matter how religious or good a person you are; you will never see the face of God.

Analyse this point and look around; how many people you know in your religion claim to see or have any solid spiritual experience in their lives. The answer will be 'None.' Any person we know is famous as a saint or saviour; they were born with natural spiritual abilities, such as; Guru Nanak, Mohammad, Jesus and many more. Once they have done their duties and gone, we name the religions after them.

It does not matter if any of these saints belonged to any religion or not; they all had one thing in common, their thoughts were universal. They loved the whole creation of God very dearly. This is why they were so close to God that it listened to their prayers. They always felt God's presence as they were standing next to it. If you come to the same state of consciousness, you can do the same; otherwise, you will never see the face of God. Good luck to you, whatever you are following.

Satnam Ji 'Live'
12.45 to 2.15 pm 28-1-2015

Today I began my meditation at 12.45 pm and I wanted to carry on forever. During meditation, I chanted the word 'Satnam-Ji.' I felt the powerful presence of Satnam Ji. I became conscious physically. I saw him standing next to my left shoulder at 1.30 pm. He stood there for a long time and

I enjoyed his company and received blessings. I noticed he was also standing on my right hand then I saw he was also standing in front of me.

When I looked within, he was also there. I noticed the time on the clock he was with me from 1.30 to 2.15 pm. I enjoyed his presence for 45 minutes. Once he was gone, then I got up from my meditation chair. I touched the ground with my hands where he was standing to show my respect.

As you know, he has been my lifeline all through. There is not a single day when I do not recite his name. Thank you, Satnam Ji.

SATNAM JI
3.20 am 7-4-2016

Today I was with Satnam Ji for a long time on the soul plane. He was sitting and I was standing in front of him. He explained how God decided to represent itself by looking like a human form on the soul plane. 'How was he created as pure Spirit and making him the in-charge of souls?

Later I was standing on the side of Satnam Ji with known Seekers. I explained to them that those very close to God or Satnam Ji, such as myself, have too many restrictions while dealing with the physical plane. We are not allowed to act like normal humans. Ethics are essential to represent Spirit on earth. Thank you, Satnam Ji.

ENLIGHTENMENT

After reading my diary, I am sure it is a time of Enlightenment for the Seekers to know; **'If I can do this, So, can you.** Before this, you had heard the stories of great saints and teachers but no one gave you hope. That this was possible for you to experience in this life. This opportunity only comes once, so make the most of it. God sent the Souls into the lower worlds for training to eventually become its' assistants. This is to share its' cause, to help other Souls, so they can have the same experience as you have done.

This is why all these Masters keep coming back, to uplift humanity spiritually. This is where most religions fail. For example, if their Master was here five hundred or two thousand years ago, the religious followers keep looking to that same teacher or name. When that Soul has done his duty for the time allotted by Spirit and has left the arena long ago. He could now be teaching through a different religion in other parts of this world.

If I look back in time, I have been here during every century and have been part of every main religion. I requested the Masters and Spirit on 23 March 2001 – 'You Can't Hide.' When my spiritual duty was not materialising, I asked Spirit to find someone else. I tell you clearly, what my request was; If my allotted duty is not materialising for any or many reasons, I will be grateful to Spirit if I can be excused this time from the present arena.

So that I can move on with my next mission, whatever part of the world it may be. We do not cling to one physical body.

On the next mission, I will be given a new one. We mean what we say. This is why we keep repeating let go of your attachments; it is not worth it. One day this will be the cause of your failure. If you want God in your life, it is never away from you but you have to be like it. Religion is Dharam in the Hindu language. Dharma is the name given to 'Spiritual Responsibility.'

You have to be God-like in your thoughts and be fair to all creation. It is well explained in all World religious scriptures. Those making a physical stand against other religions consider themselves better than others and say, you can't do this or that. I do not even consider them religious. The living Master of the time is chosen by God Itself. God entirely runs the spiritual body of the Master.

The physical Master is quite aware of many situations but cannot know everything. However, if the Master requests God, if there is something he is not aware of but wants to know, God never denies the answer. If we forget about October 1981 and again, the same happened in October 2008. I think it was done purposely by the Spirit to shift its' seat of power from America to England. I leave the conclusions for you to work out. I had been let down twice.

In 1981 I kept my silence for three reasons; Spirit may not like it if I spoke out. Second: People may not believe me. Third: I was promised by Dapren and Paul to look forward to future responsibility. At present, there are about thirty Seekers in England. Just before October 2008, I talked to about ten Seekers and out of those ten Seekers, only six believed me. Word passed around and others said, 'Dapren should have told us.'

Later, most of the members were given experiences by Spirit telling them who I am. Now, ninety percent of them have accepted me. I feel very disappointed sometimes because thousands of people have followed this path since 1965. But ten percent understood this path and only five percent followed the teachings. The others are just wasting the Master's valuable time and treating the teachings like any other religion.

Spirit took its' own course to reach me this time. No one can take this responsibility away from me until my time is up. Since Dapren passed away from this physical world, some people in America claim to be spiritual Masters. I just wonder what chair they are sitting on. I am not interested and never have been in any 'Titles.' Any Title means that one person is better or superior to the others.

I am just another Soul among all the others, just doing the job; I have been told to do so by Spirit itself. I don't know why people are fighting over these titles. There is no bigger title than God Itself. They are not God-loving people and are always in fear of losing their grip or ground. At present, I don't have any grip or ground; I am always happy. The chosen Soul, invested with God's spiritual love, becomes the centre point of this world and all universes.

Their answers will be through this Soul, whoever wants to communicate with God or Spirit. It is the spiritual side of this person that is responsible. The physical side of this person may not be aware of it because there could be one million people communicating at one time. That is why there is a veil between the spiritual and physical but he can know if any communication is required. There are no swordsmen as such, these words sound very striking to hear but there is no such thing or beings.

The only Souls representing God are the 'Nine Super Souls,' which do not carry any weapons. They have pure love; that is their strength. Some people think I am hot-tempered. That is not true. They will never know the love force I carry within. I do not blame or hold any grudge against the present leader or his organisation. They were unaware of what was happening between me and the spiritual Master. My best wishes are with them all the time and with all other religions.

We are working for the same cause of God. Spirit will choose the next living Master and I will do my best to pass over this responsibility myself. He will be fully trained spiritually over many past lives. Many people believe that if you follow the teachings for a few years and chant your spiritual 'Word,' you can become the Master. Sorry, it does not work that way. We do learn, sometimes the hard way.

Throughout my present journey, I have learned a lot and after reading my diary, I hope you have learned something. We must move on in life. Be yourself and let the others be. The opportunities in life always come; just ride along with them. It is not the end of the world. Be happy and there is no other way. I am here today but may not be here tomorrow; I will take my next assignment. What you have read in my diary may be a big thing for you but to me, it is normal.

I have been through the same situation a few centuries back, so it is normal. One thing is clear; it always happens when politics creep in from somewhere. We 'Masters' are the jokers of God. It sends us into the lower worlds to make people laugh, those who have forgotten due to their circumstances. Some we take with us, those who are ready. The rest of them can take their time. There is no time limit because God operates above matter, energy, space and Time.

We should take every instance of life positively. I have learned a lot through my physical as well as spiritual struggles. I am so glad that master-ship did not come to me as planned by Spirit earlier. Otherwise, this book never has been written. This is Enlightenment.

RUDE AWAKENING 2

God is known to be Omnipotent, Omniscient and Omnipresent. It is so powerful that it can do anything or put a veil over our senses. It was similar to previous experiences or the situations I was going through in life. It was beyond my knowledge or why? I suffered and went through serious situations a good number of times. I am not going to list my sufferings. If I do open up, you will not believe or ask, 'how can this happen to such a person as myself?

Many times, I raised the question, 'why? I often felt it was unnecessary or discouraged my sincerity towards God. I am or was aware of many things that happen in this world. A few situations could have been created for training purposes to become the future living Master. The most awaited answer of my life was given on 17 July 2018. The Spirit appeared and said that all the situations you have been through in life; **They were all created purposely.**

Then Spirit disappeared instantly. I was dumbstruck and felt so disgusted, disappointed, angry and said to myself, 'what the hell? Later I put the question to the higher spiritual authorities, 'why? And who is responsible for this?'

No answer was given. Months went by and still no response. Two years later, an answer came. You have had several spiritual guardian angels since birth. All guardians are established with your soul body to protect and create all learning situations.

As well as to control, so you do not commit such an act that the Spirit does not accept. Then, I asked for the names of guardian angels responsible for my sufferings. Up until today, I have had no answer. You can imagine my anger and due to that, I have written a few chapters expressing my disappointment. Such as God is not perfect, Guardian angels or devils and others. Any person has to pay the price to be in my position.

Again; Rude awakening 2 was done purposely. To raise anger within so that I could express this side of God. If I did not feel this anger within then, there is no way I would have preferred to write in such a manner. In history, any other spiritual person did not use or write similar words. It was another learning point for me as well. Out of this anger, **I said to God; from today onwards, I do not require any help from you. Even if I do need it, please do not help me.**

An Instant answer came; **God said; No one is helping me or if I do need help, to whom should I go?** I was dumbstruck once more and could not answer. It was a great learning point for me. I learn never to rely on anyone in life. God is working in mysterious ways to teach us. I said thank you for this valuable lesson. All through my writings, I do not write anything as nothing. All chapters are written for a purpose. This chapter is another eye-opener for me and many others.

Despite my bad, negative or suffering situations, I am still writing for God. I do not write the way others have already written or to please my readers. I had been given the task of representing God with a sparingly fresh approach. I am sure that many will appreciate my writings one day. Whatever God has given me, such as spiritual ability and authority into the higher worlds, is a lot beyond whatever I suffered.

My spiritual journey concludes that I have been playing a puppet in the hands of God. I hope I did not let God down according to its expectations and it also enjoyed my company as much as I enjoyed being obedient to God. There is only one life to live, so give it your best shot to achieve spiritual success.

God Bless All

SHER GILL Galib

London

SPIRITUAL TERMINOLOGY

Akashic Records: The total record of our physical incarnations which are kept in the causal plane. On that basis; Past, present and future can be predicted.

Angels of Death: Assistants of the king of the dead to collect the departing soul from physical at their last hour.

Astral Body: Radiant or emotional body. Astral plane; next plane above physical.

Astrology: It is the study of planets and their position concerning your date of birth, the future can be predicted.

Aura: Is a magnetic field that surrounds all souls to express their spiritual status.

Brahma: The lord of the mental plane and one of the Hindu trinity Gods. Brahma, Vishnu and Shiva.

Buddhi: Intellectual: Is part of the mind, the chief instrument of thought.

Cause & Effect: Action and reaction lead to creating negative or positive karma.

Chakra(s): Psychic centres in the human body; all yoga practitioners use these centres to have a spiritual experience.

Conscience: Is moral or ethical development in person.

Consciousness: That state of being in which the individual lives all-day

Creation: Whatever has been created by God for training purposes.

Creed (God's): All life flows from God itself; nothing can exist without spirit or the will of God.

Crown Chakra: The soft spot at the top of the human skull and easy passage for soul travel into the spiritual planes.

Cult: Is a system of worship of a Master, deity, Ideal or any celebrity.

Deja vu: Is the ability to know the events before happening.

Direct projection: It is the technique to move soul and body together instantly.

Dreams: It is a way of Spirit to communicate with all souls. The spiritual Master also communicates with Seekers, known as dream teachings.

Enlightenment: The state of spiritual knowledge and awakening within.

Eternity: Expression of life without a sense of time and space, the present spiritual dwelling is always in eternity. `

Etheric plane: The unconscious plane or dividing line between the mental and soul plane. Sub-conscious mind.

Faith: Is the keystone to having any spiritual success. It is the belief in the Master or teachings to achieve the set goal.

Free will: God's gift to each soul to decide how to create karma or live life.

Haiome: One of the most powerful spiritual **words,** it can lead the Seeker to God.

Hypnotism: One of the psychic arts to balance many disorders or to practice evil.

Imagination: It is a mental faculty to activate positive vibrations to have an inner experience or soul travel.

Immortality: It is a state of being, deathless or as opposed to mortality.

Incarnations: The continuous cycle of births and deaths in the physical world.

Individuality: The Immortal self of each soul has its own identity; no two souls are the same as twins.

Jot-Niranjan: The ruler on the astral plane and powerhouse to the physical world.

Kal: Is the overall in charge of negative Spirit.

Karma: The law of cause & effect. It is the decisive part of human suffering.

King of the Dead: Is the lord of karma on the astral plane that judges the soul's journey according to its earned karma.

Light & Sound: Are twin pillars of God or is Spirit.

Love: It is the love force of God that sustains all creation and balance of all universes. There is human love and impersonal love.

Magic: It is trickery or part of an illusion to please the audience.

Manifestation: Manifested, which is normally apparent to the physical senses.

Meditation: Is the practice of sitting while reciting spiritual **word** for esoteric experience.

Mental plane: This is the fourth plane in God's world. The sound is of 'running water'.

Mind: The thinking part of human consciousness or the chief instrument for the soul's survival in the lower worlds.

Ocean of love and Mercy: Life-giving spirit. Love, for the wellbeing of all creation.

Omnipotence: All-powerful. omniscience; all-knowing. Omnipresent; present.

Par-Brahm: He is the lord on the etheric plane.

Para-Vidya: Is spiritual knowledge. **Apara**-vidya; is physical knowledge.

Philosophy: It is the psychic or core study of the religions by use of the mental faculties.

Physical plane: This is the lowest plane of matter, energy, space and time.

Power: There is supreme or neuter power and negative & positive operates in the lower worlds. Political or any other authority in this world is also power.

Prayers: This is an approach to contacting a spiritual Master or God. It could be a request or to feel its presence. If you know God is within, it will understand your needs.

Prophecy: Spiritual man who can forecast future events long before they happen.

Psychic Space: It is the natural right of each soul to feel free. Be yourself and let the others be.

Re-incarnation: It is the circle of each soul, birth- death and rebirth.

Religions: Are spiritual and social systems created in the name of a religious guru.

Sach Khand: Is in the fifth plane of God's world. It is the first pure spirit plane and the ruler is Satnam.

Sahasara-Dal-Kanwal: The capital city of the astral plane and meeting place between the Master and Seeker after sun & moon worlds.

Satnam Ji: The first personification of God to be seen in male form. Humans are created, replicas of Satnam Ji. Lord of soul plane. The sound is of a single-note flute.

Satya-Yuga: Golden age: This yuga lasted for 1,728,000 years.

Seeker: Disciple: Who has the yearning within to experience God in this lifetime.

Self-realisation: Knowledge of its existence as soul and having answers to self, such as; Who am I? Where am I going after death and how to reach there?

Self-Surrender: Complete submission to the Master and the principles of teachings you follow.

Soul: Atma: Is a unit of God-awareness. It is a micro part of the macro.

Soul Travel: Is the change in the state of consciousness or the means of travelling to other planes.

Space and Time: Space means nothing apart from our perception of objects and time means nothing apart from our experience of events.

Spirit: It is the combination of light and sound. It is the adhesive or life force of all universes.

Spiritual Freedom: Is liberation from the lower worlds or the wheel of eighty-four.

Spiritual unfoldment: This is to become aware of what God has invested within us.

Spirituality: Is the essence of spiritual experience, which cannot be taught but can be caught.

Sub-conscious mind: The unconscious or the reactive mind.

Sufism: Is Islamic mysticism and total dedication to Allah.

Total awareness: It is the ultimate goal for all spiritual Seekers to achieve on this path.

Trinity of God: God, Spirit and the Master. Father, Son and Holy ghost.

Truth: Is the only source of knowledge and man is the mirror of truth. You cannot receive more than what your soul can hold.

Vibrations: Spiritual waves we carry as our aura will show on our countenance.

Will of God: Is God's ultimate decision and nothing can exist without this will of God.

Will power: Indicates the maturity of each person. The strength of execution.

Wisdom: Is spiritual knowledge beyond all intellectual ability.

Word of God: Shabda, spirit or the flow of spirit from God.

Lightning Source UK Ltd.
Milton Keynes UK
UKHW040739020123
414708UK00001B/42